TIME IS
RUNNING
OUT

SAVE THE WORLD—

BEFORE IT'S TOO LATE

REINHARD BONNKE

Regal

A Division of Gospel Light
Ventura, California, U.S.A.

PUBLISHED BY REGAL BOOKS
A DIVISION OF GOSPEL LIGHT
VENTURA, CALIFORNIA, U.S.A.
PRINTED IN U.S.A.

Regal Books is a ministry of Gospel Light, an evangelical Christian publisher dedicated to serving the local church. We believe God's vision for Gospel Light is to provide church leaders with biblical, user-friendly materials that will help them evangelize, disciple and minister to children, youth and families.

It is our prayer that this Regal book will help you discover biblical truth for your own life and help you meet the needs of others. May God richly bless you.

For a free catalog of resources from Regal Books and Gospel Light, please call your Christian supplier, or contact us at 1-800-4-GOSPEL.

Cover Design by Kevin Keller
Interior Design by Robert Williams
Edited by Douglas Shaw and David Webb

LIBRARY OF CONGRESS CATALOGING-IN-PUBLICATION DATA
Bonnke, Reinhard.
        Time is running out / Reinhard Bonnke.
            p.   cm.
        Includes bibliographical references.
        ISBN 0-8307-2466-4 (trade paper)
        1. Evangelistic work.   I. Title.
        BV3790.B57   1999   99-046141
        269'.2—dc21

1   2   3   4   5   6   7   8   9   10   11   12   13   14   15   /   06   05   04   03   02   01   00   99

Rights for publishing this book in other languages are contracted by Gospel Literature International (GLINT). GLINT also provides technical help for the adaptation, translation and publishing of Bible study resources and books in scores of languages worldwide. For further information, write to GLINT at P.O. Box 4060, Ontario, CA 91761-1003, U.S.A. You may also send E-mail to Glintint@aol.com, or visit the GLINT web site at www.glint.org.

CONTENTS

PREFACE

In November 1996, the Regent University School of Divinity was privileged to receive German evangelist Reinhard Bonnke on campus to deliver a series of lectures on world evangelization. He was asked to prepare his lectures drawing from his perspective as the prominent crusade evangelist of the previous decade.

The university was on tiptoe with expectation as he came to deliver this historic series. One of the largest classes in the history of the university gathered in the Moot Court of Robertson Hall to hear Bonnke deliver many hours of inspiring teaching. In the evenings, after teaching most of the day, Bonnke preached in the Parkway Temple Church to standing-room-only crowds.

Now Bonnke has adapted his historic lectures for publication. This book gathers together and distills the biblical vision of Reinhard Bonnke to reach the masses for Jesus Christ in this generation. Bonnke exists on the cutting edge of evangelism. His African crusades have drawn as many as 500,000 persons in one service. His gospel preaching with signs and wonders following has amazed the world and brought millions into the kingdom of Jesus Christ. In his wake, churches have exploded with new growth and the powers of darkness have been exposed and defeated.

Now it is my hope that this work adapted from the Regent University lectures of Reinhard Bonnke will take its place as a major resource for future generations in much the same way that Charles G. Finney's lectures on "Revivals of Religion" served to inspire earlier generations to trust God for mighty movings of the Holy Spirit.

VINSON SYNAN
Dean of the School of Divinity
Regent University
Virginia Beach, Virginia

TIME IS OF THE ESSENCE!

If 10,000 people live near your church, according to statistics 4 of them die each week. Is it satisfactory, then, if only 1 of the 10,000 is saved every month, or even every week? I find it is impossible to exaggerate the urgency of sharing the gospel! The greatest work on earth is to preach the good news, and the greatest need in the world is the need for the gospel.

The world is in critical condition, desperate for the transforming power of Christ; meanwhile the devil schemes to hide this obvious fact from us. His policies of murder and genocide having failed to prevent the birth of our Savior (see Matt. 2:16-18) and later, His resurrection, Satan's only other alternative was to prevent the preaching of the gospel.

At first, the devil used mainly persecution and false gospels to this end, but over the centuries he has built up a considerable armory. A favorite subtle weapon he deploys is to redirect our priorities. Satan doesn't mind how hard we work for our churches, as long as our work keeps us from wreaking havoc on his evil kingdom by spreading the gospel.

Beware! We can study doctrine, engage in fellowship, preach prosperity or cultivate our own souls in ways that bring us no closer to fulfilling Christ's commission to preach the gospel to every nation. Let us not be fooled. We are wallowing in deception when we allow "good" activities to crowd out the most urgent work of all.

Gasping for the Gospel

Every unredeemed life cries out for the gospel, like a fish on the riverbank gasping for water. Many in the world have given up hope. They have seen the limits of science, technology, medicine, politics and education, and they turn to opiates to forget—drugs, drink, religious mysticism. Like the mythical hydra, evil grows two heads for every one that we cut off. This monster needs the dagger of the cross of Christ plunged into its heart.

Only the gospel can cure the woes of the globe. To not preach the gospel means that we hide the medicine from the patient! Isaiah observed, "The whole head is sick, and the whole heart faints" (Isa. 1:5, *NKJV*). Sometimes our bodies cure themselves, but very often medicines are needed. When it comes to salvation, though, there is no other curative for man except the supernatural power of the gospel. Your task and mine is to put that wonderful remedy on the table. One can never force a cure on somebody, not even by threat, if the patient resolves not to take it. People who refuse the gospel will simply die, unless God in His mercy intervenes.

Why Humanity Suffers

When I am interviewed by the media, one of the questions I am most frequently asked is: Why does God allow so much suffering in the world? I have often pondered this question myself, perhaps not for the reasons that jaded reporters ask it, but because I genuinely suffer when I see others suffering. So, why does God allow suffering? You may just as well ask the U.S. Secretary of Transportation why he allows accidents on the highways. No doubt, he would take exception to the implied accusation of your question, pointing to the well-defined rules of the road. "Every time a law is broken," he might reply, "the offender places himself and others in danger. Accidents and suffering occur as a result."

People suffer for chiefly one reason: They have chosen to ignore God's rule book, the Bible, and everything has gone terribly wrong as a result. Our loving Creator knows exactly how we have been made and what will harm us. Consequently, with a caring, protective heart He says, "You shall not —." His commandments are not dictatorial edicts designed to spoil our fun; rather they are the Manufacturer's handling instructions. God knows that our psyches cannot handle sin and that we are actually crushed and tormented by our own misdeeds. Few would argue against the wisdom of reading the instruction manual before using a new appliance. People take care not to break a tape recorder or a new washing machine, but strangely, many don't seem to mind destroying their own spirits and souls with the poison of sin.

Do you begin to see more clearly the desperate need for the gospel and why God's heart cry that we share the truth is so insistent, so urgent?

The Prodigal Planet

The supreme wonder of the gospel is its present realization of life—life of such unfathomable and enduring quality that it cannot fade for all eternity. Other religions may claim to have the answers to the present misery of the individual, but what does it profit a man to achieve harmony with nature yet lose his soul?

Jesus offers eternal life now! Jesus said, "I am the resurrection and the life. He who believes in me will live, even though he dies; and whoever lives and believes in me will never die" (John 11:25,26). Urgent? The world needs His precious gift of eternal life *now*.

When God made the world, He filled it with an inexhaustible supply of the purest of pleasures. Every wonder, taste and delight came from the loving heart of God for His children. And when we walk in God's way, the world is all ours. But when we resist Him, we hinder His glorious plans for our lives and turn our backs on His good gifts.

The human race has achieved brilliance in the art and science of annihilation. Mass killings of children in our schools and state-sanctioned abortion clinics; scenes of carnage, both real and imagined, on our TV screens; the wanton devastation of the natural environment; the ongoing testing of weapons of mass destruction—all around us is clear evidence of the ravages of sin. We war, we hate, we trample on the fair earth and foul all that He has given us.

This is what comes of turning away from God. Most of man's ills are man-made. Yet there is power in the gospel to reverse these fatal processes. The truth shall set us free, calling us back to do His will, which is always for the good of us all. God loves His prodigal planet, and if we return, we shall enjoy the glad welcome of the Father.

I Have Seen It Happen!

God is now mightily sweeping parts of the world with the gospel, making the way for salvation. I have seen sins forgiven, racial harmony achieved, crime eradicated, marriages restored, families reunited, evil men turned into saints, addicts freed, the fatally ill cured and many other miraculous healings.

Many times following our evangelistic campaigns in Africa, local police have reported a sudden and dramatic decrease in crime. People's lives are being changed! I'll never forget how, in the nation of Burkina Faso, many large items—stolen refrigerators and other household furnishings—were brought to the preaching field by repentant people who wanted to cleanse their homes of stolen property. The police had to come and haul the items away in several trucks! This glorious scene has been repeated in many other countries.

The gospel gives to all who will receive the dignity of sons and daughters of God. Men who once were savages are reclaimed and walk as princes. Hallelujah! What a reason to preach the gospel! Could anything be more thrilling, adventurous and worthwhile? What else is worth your life's effort?

Nothing less than the salvation of this world is at stake. Certainly, Jesus did not think it a waste of His time to heal the sick and feed the feckless multitudes. He invited persecution for healing the man with a withered arm, and from that moment on, He walked with a price on His head (see Matt. 12:10-13). But that man mattered to Jesus, and his arm had to be restored, no matter what the personal cost to the Son of Man.

Reflections of Reality

Why is music so precious to so many? When we are touched by inspired music, often we receive a glimpse of the eternal. Music only suggests infinity, however; the melody echoes a faraway greatness that it cannot fulfill. That infinity is God Himself, and what music only suggests is given to us when we receive salvation through Jesus Christ and begin to worship Him.

God is our natural habitat. In Him we move and have our being. Until we hear and obey the gospel, until we find Him, we remain caged. Men and women everywhere are beating their heads against prison bars forged by their own materialism and unbelief. Their very money holds them captive. Deep calls to deep and height to height within our souls. Our art, our poetry, our works of beauty are but expressions of imprisoned creatures who dimly remember the glories of the free air and the mountains. While good in themselves, these expressions remain mere reflections of reality. Jesus is the reality behind all that we see or do. His gospel releases us from bondage, allowing us to come into our true element, our intended heritage!

Until they find and accept the truth, the inhabitants of this world will wander the wastes of the wilderness, scanning the horizons where dawn never breaks, looking for the elusive elixir of happiness. Unbelievers extract what drink they can from the dry ground of resentment, doubt and hatred. But the Spirit and the Bride say, "Come! Whoever is thirsty, let him come; and whoever wishes, let him take the free gift of the water of life" (Rev. 22:17).

A way of life is preached in the gospel that leads ever onward to the perfect day. Do we need any more reason to preach the gospel?

The Second Coming

They asked him, "Lord, are you at this time going to restore the kingdom to Israel?" He said to them, "It is not for you to know the times or dates the Father has set by His own authority" (Acts 1:6,7).

He was taken up before their very eyes, and a cloud hid him from their sight. They were looking intently up into the sky as he was going, when suddenly two men dressed in white stood beside them. "Men of Galilee," they said, "why do you stand here looking into the sky? This same Jesus, who has been taken from you into heaven, will come back in the same way you have seen him go into heaven" (Acts 1:9-11).

Jesus often talked to His disciples about the Kingdom, so naturally they asked questions about it. They wanted to know when it would come and whether Israel would be returned to its place in the sun. Jesus told them such matters were not to concern them, but said, "You will be my witnesses in Jerusalem, and in all Judea and Samaria, and to the ends of the earth" (Acts 1:8). They were asking Jesus when *He* would do something; He turned it around and told them *they* must do something.

The disciples' job was to witness, not to worry about times and seasons. They knew the prophecies they had read in Daniel and in other books, and the angels reminded them there would come a day when Christ would return. So the disciples went out and preached the gospel, and the return of Jesus became part of the substance of their message to the world.

There is a difference between preaching the return of Jesus and working out times and dates when it will happen. Throughout two millennia, and even today, there have been hundreds of predictions. In studying prophecy, people have concerned themselves with times and dates, taking this or that verse and building speculations around it. They have made quite a minor science out of interpreting prophecies and called it eschatology. Neat blueprints of the future have been drawn up. Books have laid out the divine program for the future with everything recorded in eye-catching charts and graphs. In 1930, a book was written about Christ's coming entitled *The World's Next Great*

Event. In fact, the world's next great event was World War II. This kind of calculation and analysis has only served to dull the Church's witness to Jesus' return.

The cry that should go forth is: "Behold, the bridegroom is coming" (Matt. 25:6, *NKJV*) and "Behold! The Lamb of God who takes away the sin of the world!" (John 1:29, *NKJV*). Our constant responsibility until the very moment of His appearing is to give our time, our money, our effort to the task Jesus set before us: "You will be my witnesses."

Why do we stand here looking into the sky? Let us get on with it! There isn't a moment to lose. Jesus is coming soon!

THE RELUCTANT EVANGELIST

There was once a tribe that worshiped the moon. "The moon shines at night," they explained, "when it is dark and we need light. But the silly old sun shines during the day, when there's plenty of light." What could be more pointless?

Of course there is light during the day because the sun shines, and there is light in America because the gospel light shines here. But there are many places in the world where it is very dark. I suppose I've been like the moon, trying to bring light to the dark places of the earth. When Paul preached in Troas all night and Eutychus fell asleep, "there were many lamps in the upstairs room" where he was talking (Acts 20:8). There are many shining lamps in America today. And that includes every Christian in America who reads this book. *You* are called to be shining as lights in the midst of a crooked generation, not hiding your light under a bushel (see Matt. 5:15; Mark 4:21; Luke 11:33).

Some people shine intellectually and speak brilliantly. I am
just an ordinary evangelist, although I do believe the evangelist's
job is the most important in the world. My natural environment
is a platform in a field somewhere in Africa, not speaking at a
university or sitting at a typewriter. Any brightness on my part in
the pages that follow must come from the Holy Spirit and the
Word of God. My hope is the promise in Daniel 12:3: "Those
who lead many to righteousness, [will shine] like the stars for
ever and ever."

God's Message for the Church

People ask me what God is saying to the church. He is saying what
He has always said: "Preach the gospel to every creature" (Mark
16:15, *NKJV*). If Jesus Himself were to take my place here in these
last days before the final judgment, He would repeat His last words
to the disciples in Acts 1:8: "You will receive power when the Holy
Spirit comes on you; and you will be my witnesses in Jerusalem,
and in all Judea and Samaria, and to the ends of the earth." Until
we have done that, He has no further instructions for us.

It has been suggested that there should be a moratorium on
bringing more converts into the Church until the Church is fit
and ready to receive them. If that were possible in a period of,
say, a week or so, I might agree. But how can we ever hope to be
fit if we stop obeying Christ? His command to us is to bring in
converts.

Though spiritual training and discipleship are vital, concen-
trating on our own holiness as our primary focus will never
make us fit to reach others with the gospel. Certainly, Jesus calls
us to be holy, but outreach to the world is part of sanctification.
Sanctification does not take place in seclusion only; holiness
requires that we look outward to the spiritually lost.

I know of no finer way to develop spirituality than to go all out to win others for Christ. When we try to reach people with the gospel, we know that we have to be real. Evangelism should be the thought, the impetus behind every agenda, if we want a church that is alive. When church boards downplay evangelism, how can they keep the church from stagnation and sterility? If the people of God do not view their overall purpose as winning people for Christ, they become just listeners, sermon tasters, choir critics or leadership judges. The church is not a restaurant for spiritual gourmets cultivating a discriminating palate for food from the pulpit. It is a canteen for workers. With a job to do, church members have no time to criticize. A horse which fulfills its role by pulling its load never kicks.

The Aim of the Church

The primary aim of every church service—prayer meetings, Bible studies, young people's meetings, choir practices, communion services—should be evangelistic. Why shouldn't every service be open to outsiders? Especially at communion, when the emblems of bread and wine are taken, we should make sure the church is *full* of the godless. That cup of red wine is the greatest preacher in the world. It is the gospel in a cup—an opportunity to invite lost sinners to accept the sacrifice of the Cross. Some churches exclude outsiders from communion. What a lost opportunity! The precious blood of Jesus cleanses us from all sin. Shall only the clean come to the fountain?

If a church has tried and failed in its attempts at evangelism, it is time for a serious reevaluation of its efforts. Evangelism demands the most intensive thinking. The finance committee's job is saving souls, not saving money. Any surplus funds should go into the true business of the church: saving the world.

Predestination and Evangelism

Predestination, the controversial doctrine that every believer has been preselected by God regardless of our evangelistic efforts, is an academic subject for high theological discussion. My approach, however, is not to get bogged down in theory but to do the work of an evangelist. My response to the long-standing debate? Cut through the polemics and step out in action.

Whether people are among the "elect" or not, I want to make certain that every man, woman and child has heard the gospel. I am not going to risk the eternal destiny of any souls based upon doctrinal deductions or theories. There is nothing in the New Testament that says we should not preach the gospel and nothing to say we should not do our best to persuade folk into the Kingdom. So that's what I do.

We shall know the truth only when we get to heaven. If everybody I find there was predestined, that's fine. But I surely do not want anyone in heaven to say to me, "Did you know for certain I was elected? Why didn't you preach the gospel to me? You gambled on your ideas being right and played dice with my soul. I could have been in hell instead of here."

The Reluctant Evangelist

If you read through the Bible beginning at Genesis, you will find nothing said about evangelism until you get to the little book of Jonah, a book which stands out from the rest of the Bible. It is almost the evangelist's *vade mecum*, a personal handbook for daily use.

Though most people are acquainted with Jonah, many (including some Christians) don't believe the story presented in this book. They think there's something fishy about the story of

Jonah. However, Jesus and His contemporaries regarded it as history, not as a fable or even a parable. And whoever wrote down the story of Jonah knew how to write. This small book deserves our close attention.

The prophet Jonah lived about 800 years before Christ. He heard the call of God to go to Nineveh, the last capital city of the Assyrian Empire. It stood on the river Tigris, 600 miles as the crow flies due east from where Jonah lived. Instead of going to Nineveh, however, Jonah bought passage on a ship to Tarshish—that is, heading west—in the other direction. He was desperate to get away from his obligation; Nineveh was the last place he wanted to go.

Note the way Jonah's flight is described. Jonah 1:3 says he went *down* to Joppa. Then he went *down* into the ship, and then *down* into the ship's hold (v. 5). Then when a storm came, the sailors threw Jonah *down* into the sea, and a great fish swallowed him and he went *down* into the belly of the big fish. He must have felt down, all right—down in the mouth. He then prayed, saying to the Lord, "You hurled me into the deep. I went *down* to the moorings of the mountains" (Jon. 2:3,6, *NKJV*). When the fish vomited Jonah and God spoke, the text says, "Jonah arose" (3:3, *NKJV*). *Going to preach when God sends us is elevating—we arise!*

Let's have a little sympathy for Jonah, for Nineveh had a fearsome reputation. One or two of their kings were decidedly brutal, some of the worst to ever walk the earth. They took pleasure in atrocities and cruelties so monstrous that they shock us even now. If I were to describe them you likely wouldn't sleep tonight, and if you did, this is the stuff of nightmares. Jonah certainly didn't relish the thought of a confrontation with men like that. How could a foreigner hope to preach against them and come out alive? Of course, he did eventually go and Nineveh actually repented of its wicked ways. Jonah's preaching seems to have been effective.

Yet Jonah was perturbed by the end results. He wanted to see the judgment of God fall on Nineveh, and who could blame him? He had warned the city that God was about to destroy it. Their wickedness had reached the ears of God and judgment was what they deserved. But the city repented and God withheld his judgment, at least for a period of time. Less than 200 years later Nineveh was totally destroyed.

Jonah's Profound Insight

Now here is the real point of Jonah's story, and it speaks to every evangelist who ever went out to do God's work. Jonah had preached judgment and no judgment came. That was just what he had feared would happen. In fact, Jonah had never wanted to preach against the city, for the very reason that if his preaching were successful, God would change His mind about judgment! Afterwards, he railed against God, saying, "O, LORD, is this not what I said when I was still at home? That is why I was so quick to flee to Tarshish. I knew that you are a gracious and compassionate God, slow to anger and abounding in love, a God who relents from sending calamity" (Jon. 4:2).

Jonah had profound insight into the character of God. In all 39 books of the Old Testament, this statement of the prophet stands out as something exceptional. Jonah knew God had a heart of unparalleled goodness. More than that, he knew that the mercies of the Lord extended beyond the borders of Israel into enemy territory, embracing even the Gentiles. Few in Israel would have believed this could be true. In that age of spiritual darkness, only the Holy Spirit could have shown this to the prophet. He somehow knew God could be as gracious with Gentiles as with Israel, even with the worst sinners on earth. That is why he went—and why he didn't want to go. Part of him wanted this wicked nation to get what it really deserved, but at the same time he knew God was not like that. Jonah wanted vengeance, but God was—and is—a God of forgiveness.

Jonah knew the compassion of God but had no compassion himself. Any man who stands up to speak of Christ knows very well what Jonah knew. It is common knowledge among the saved that God is loving, gracious, merciful and compassionate. But do we personally harbor such feelings for the lost? Jonah had none at all; he preached only out of duty or obedience. There could not be a more serious shortcoming for any evangelist or anybody who preaches the Word of God. Evangelism is not a matter of simply mouthing words of God's pitying love or spelling out theology. An evangelist's heart should beat in tune with the heartbeat of God, expressive of His heart's longings and compassion.

The need in evangelism is twofold: the truth and people who reflect it. Some people say that "preaching the right thing" is enough. It is not. The Holy Spirit has a part in this, placing the missing ingredient in our own hearts: "God has poured out his love into our hearts by the Holy Spirit, whom he has given us" (Rom. 5:5). The love of God in Christ is more than a piece of systematic theology, and it is meant to come alive in those who declare it. We can preach with tongues of fire when we have His fire in our bellies. How do you get those fires burning? Get to know the Word of God for yourself. It is God's Word to *you*.

Jonah was a rare preacher and prophet in that he didn't *want* to succeed. He hoped nobody in Nineveh would take notice of the message he preached. Yet even the king on his throne became alarmed about his sins and decided to do something about it. If we take the Word of God upon our lips, we should know what we are doing. This is major firepower that no one should "play" with.

Beyond Israel: A World Vision for the Lost

Among the Old Testament prophets, Jonah was the only one to leave Israel and actually preach the word of the Lord openly in the streets of a foreign land. There was a kinship of spirit between Jonah and Jesus. Jonah was the only prophet with whom Jesus personally associated Himself. He spoke of him as *the* sign to Israel (see Matt. 12:39). Jonah had a God-given burden for a Gentile city. The next to carry such a burden was Jesus Christ Himself. His heart was big enough to hold the whole of Israel and the whole Gentile world.

No other prophet of Israel ever carried the word of the Lord to the outside world except when they themselves were carried away as captives of war. In Babylon, some maintained their witness to the Lord, the God of Israel. We read of these in the books of Daniel and Esther. But the northern tribes were absorbed in the Assyrian Empire and lost. In Psalm 137, we are told, "Our captors asked us for songs . . . they said 'Sing us one of the songs of Zion!'" But their reply was "How can we sing the songs of the LORD while in a foreign land?" (see Ps. 137:3,4). What a pity. Those songs could have introduced the living God to the outside world.

The concern of God for His creatures extends to all equally, even to the most renegade and wicked. However, Jonah didn't feel the same way at all and was out of sympathy with his commission. He tried to get away from God. But God was determined he should go and sent the storm at sea as Jonah tried to flee. It was God's storm of protest at Jonah's attitude, devoid of any pity.

God made Jonah a remarkable exception. He coerced him into doing what Israel was supposed to do but never did. God raised up Israel to make the name of the Lord known throughout the whole earth (see Ps. 67, 96; Ezek. 36:23). Even the original

Church was entirely Jewish for maybe 20 years. Perhaps Jonah was, despite his shortcomings, one of the greatest of all the prophets.

Evangelism Is God's Initiative

The initiative to save Nineveh came from God, not from Jonah. For God desires not the death of any man, but that all should repent (see 2 Pet. 3:9). The initiative for evangelism comes from God, and God both calls and equips us for this work. It was He who gave some to be evangelists (see Eph. 4:11). At first, Jonah acted on his own initiative and went in the opposite direction, west to Tarshish instead of going east, and God responded by sending a ferocious storm. God has promised to bless and support His own divine plans. There is no blessing upon our own plans.

So where was Jonah going? Where is Tarshish? Various experts have studied this, trying to find out. The word *tarshish* is linked closely with the smelting of ore, silver, gold and tin. The ships of Tarshish were treasure ships, famous for the expensive cargo they carried. They became symbols of wealth, power and pride. For Jonah, Nineveh represented only sacrifice. It was a stark choice: Nineveh with its menace or Tarshish with its money?

Are you and I "for hire" where the biggest salary is offered? Is cash to be the deciding factor in our careers? Mammon and ministry don't mix too well. He profits most who serves best.

God Is There, No Matter Where You Run

Aboard the ship to Tarshish, the crew did not know Jonah was a prophet, nor did they know his God. The sailors were heathens, but they rebuked the prophet of God for sleeping on the job. "How can you sleep?" they said to him in the midst of the storm.

"Get up and call on your god! Maybe he will take notice of us, and we will not perish" (Jon. 1:6).

The people of this world expect a prophet to speak up, whether they agree with what he says or not. Maybe they don't want to adopt Christian morals or the way of the Lord for themselves, yet they still believe morality is a good thing for other people to practice. If we don't preach what they know we believe, they feel cheated, let down. The Church must never fail to sound a clear note on what is right and wrong.

When backed into a corner, Jonah admitted who he was. This startled and even terrified the crew. These men were potential converts; they already recognized the power and authority of God. Despite Jonah's poor testimony, they came to believe in Jonah's God: "At this the men greatly feared the LORD, and they offered a sacrifice to the LORD and made vows to him" (Jon. 1:16).

Here was a man who knew the marvelous truth about God, and yet they had to ask him who his God was. With Jonah aboard their ship, who his God was should have been clear. Do people who know who your God is?

It is a striking thing that God's identity is linked to men. He was first known through the life of Abraham and was called the God of Abraham. The world's ideas about God came first from seeing what sort of man Abraham was. His life portrayed his God and served as a recommendation for Him.

When Jacob first fled from home and from the murderous threats of Esau, he referred to the Lord as the God of his fathers, Abraham and Isaac. That is how he identified God, by how their God had shaped their lives. This brought a sense of awe upon Jacob. He resolved that one day their God would be his God (see Gen. 28:21). He didn't feel that could be a reality until his own life reflected his God. If the name of Jacob was to be associated with his fathers' God, he wanted to maintain the reputation of that God.

Evangelism means that somebody will say "I believe in my mother's God" or "I believe in Jack's God" or "Jean's God." People talk about presenting the gospel in a nutshell, but it can actually only be presented in a person. The gospel is more than a formula for getting to heaven when you die. The gospel offers life, not just a life belt. The essence of evangelism is to *show* what God is like.

Jesus told His disciples the Spirit of God is the Spirit of witness (see John 15:26). Today, we often talk about "power evangelism"—signs and wonders to confirm the gospel. But Jesus said that even wicked people would work miracles though He never knew them (see Matt. 7:22,23). Paul also talked about the demonstration of the Spirit (see 1 Cor. 2:4). However, one cannot help but be impressed by the way the apostle manifested the reality of the gospel in his daily life. He told the Corinthians that their lives were epistles "known and read by everybody" (2 Cor. 3:2). Looking at us, will people be able to say, "So, that is what your God is like"?

The True Spirit of Evangelism

Evangelism means to recommend Jesus. The evangelistic method taught by Jesus was that we should recommend Him, by our lives as well as by our words. We should be "Jesus people," or more precisely, "Jesus-of-the-Gospels people."

We are the light of the world; there are no other options (see Matt. 5:14). Jonah fled from the presence of the Lord, but he carried a light in his soul that somehow shone through. He concealed his testimony from the captain and crew of the ship that he boarded at Joppa. But Jonah knew God, and that came across even when he tried to run away from God. The crew of a storm-tossed ship sensed it and caught the vision.

Jonah knew in his very bones what God was like: He was gracious. How could he, Jonah, preach judgment to Nineveh when he knew perfectly well that God was so kind and merciful? He would forgive their wickedness at the drop of a hat, or rather at the first sign of repentance. So he fled from the presence of the Lord (see Jon. 1:3). To be where God was meant carrying the scent of grace in his clothes. The atmosphere was infected by compassion, and Jonah did not want to feel compassionate. He had no inclination for smiling kindly toward monsters like the lords of Nineveh.

Evangelism means deliverance from judgment. But Jonah strongly felt that Nineveh deserved judgment. His attitude was understandable, I suppose. Jonah's feelings are often echoed in the book of Psalms (see, for example, Ps. 18:37-42).

When Jesus was traveling through Samaria with His disciples, He wanted to stay one night in a village. But the local inhabitants were hostile to the Jews and would not accommodate the party. The disciples had been enjoying the experience of using God's power to heal by the authority vested in them by Jesus. They knew Elijah had brought fire down from heaven upon soldiers sent to arrest him (see 2 Kings 1:8-14), so they proposed doing the same to wipe out this village. After all, God had done it to Sodom and Gomorrah. But Jesus said to them, "You do not know what manner of spirit you are of. For the Son of Man did not come to destroy men's lives but to save them" (Luke 9:55,56, NKJV).

John the Baptist had a similar problem. He preached the fire of judgment. He came in the spirit and power of Elijah. He said: "You brood of vipers! Who warned you to flee from the coming wrath? The ax is already at the root of the trees, and every tree that does not produce good fruit will be cut down and thrown into the fire. His winnowing fork is in his hand to clear his threshing floor and to gather the wheat into his barn, but he will burn up the chaff with unquenchable fire" (Luke 3:7,9,17). That is so much like the preaching of the fiery Elijah that it sounds ironic when Luke adds, "With many other words John exhorted the people and preached the good news to them" (3:18)! Good news? Hell fire?!

John later saw Jesus at work and saw no flaming judgments fall. He sent to ask Jesus if he had identified the wrong man as Messiah. Jesus sent back the messengers to describe the mercies of God among the afflicted and dying and to deliver a message: "Blessed is the man who does not fall away on account of me" (Luke 7:23).

LOVE IS THE TRUE SPIRIT OF EVANGELISM.
WE SHOULD WARN PEOPLE ABOUT THE
DANGER OF HELL AS IF THEY WERE OUR
OWN CHILDREN WALKING ON THE BRINK
OF A VOLCANO.

Elijah was the scourge of Baal and Jezebel and her pathetic husband, Ahab. Jesus did not come as a scourge. He bared His *own* back to the scourge, not ours. He showed to us the ultimate reality behind the universe, a heart beating with infinite longing and concern over every one of His creatures. In fact, the more sunken in the pit the people were, the more He bled for them.

That kind of love is the true Spirit of evangelism.

I know people are going to hell, and if I care about them I should warn them. But I should warn them as if they were my own children walking on the brink of a volcano. Hatred should not be present in our preaching. Our mission is compassion. Because hell opens its mouth to devour sinners, we should feel the greater anxiety for their souls. We can't gloat in satisfaction and shout for joy over sinners in hell. Warnings are one thing, threats another. Jonah found it difficult to preach; he enjoyed preaching wrath but knew that God did not enjoy being angry. God is longsuffering.

The Voice of Love

I have often wondered how Jesus sounded when He spoke. Once Jesus pronounced seven woes against certain cities (see Rev. 2:1–3:22). But I wonder, what was His tone of voice? I imagine He spoke these judgments with a voice of sorrow. What love filled His voice, what tears filled His eyes, even when He went to Jerusalem to be rejected (see Matt. 23:37)! His heart would show in His tone of voice. What kind of tone did those privileged people hear?

In Luke 4:22 we read that they "were amazed at the gracious words that came from his lips." The Temple police were sent to arrest Jesus. They came back spellbound and disarmed. They said, "No one ever spoke the way this man does" (John 7: 46). How did Jesus sound when He cried, "Father, forgive them, for they do not know what they are doing" (Luke 23:34)?

D. L. Moody once spoke in London to an invited audience of a thousand or so rationalists. The meeting was fiercely hostile, but Moody literally sobbed, with tears running down his beard, as he pleaded with them to turn to Christ. Suddenly the meeting broke and hundreds turned to Christ. Those people were never the same again.

I don't mean that the gospel should be turned into sob stuff, a tearjerker. The voice of Jesus did far more than stir people's emotions. Their reaction was not tears but joy. He told His disciples that he spoke to give them peace and joy (see John 14:27; 15:11). In fact there was no pathos in the words or teaching of Jesus, nothing that people today would call syrupy-sweet sentimentalism. The gospel sound should be triumphant, certain, with a note of gladness.

That is, of course, a long way from and in stark contrast to the warning voice of Jonah in doomed Nineveh, but grace and truth came to light through Jesus Christ. There is no bell that rings as loudly as love.

Righteous Anger and Right Priorities

God would speak to Jonah through a plant that grew up over him and then withered. Jonah was staying outside the city for a while, waiting to see what would happen. The sun was very hot and so Jonah had made himself a shelter. A plant provided by God grew up over Jonah to give him even more protection from the heat, but then it withered overnight. Its root had been destroyed by some kind of worm (see Jon. 4:7).

Jonah was furious. God said, "Do you have a right to be angry about this plant?" Well, Jonah thought he did. He claimed to be angry enough to die (v. 9). So God stated His case. The last words of the book of Jonah are the words of the Lord:

> You have been concerned about this vine, though you did not tend it or make it grow. It sprang up overnight and died overnight. But Nineveh has more than a hundred and twenty thousand people who cannot tell their right hand from their left, and many cattle as well. Should I not be concerned about that great city? (Jon. 4:10,11).

To Jonah, the plant seemed more important than the lives of people. This has a lesson to teach us about what is important to us. There are plenty of righteous causes around today. The United States is particularly known abroad for its powerful lobbies affecting legislation on several great moral issues, such as concern for the environment. Some Christians may find themselves involved in such matters politically or even professionally, and why not? The question is, what are we choosing to be most angry about?

Social, environmental and moral issues are not trifles to be dismissed lightly. We ought to be angry about many of the abominations perpetrated by modern society. *But what about the issue of eternal salvation?* Pro-life people fight (rightly) for the life of unborn babies, but what are we doing about the souls of the millions of people walking our city streets?

We cannot all be preachers or evangelists. There must be people who do all sorts of different jobs that keep society and our churches functioning. Yet whatever our concern with the fabric of mortal life and the issues of society, *the call of Christ to preach the gospel to all creatures must still be our ultimate objective.*

To put it another way, we can be like Jonah, whose most immediate problem was the loss of shade that had been provided by his now-dead plant—or so he thought. Are we more disturbed about endangered species in the North Atlantic than by the eternal danger in which Christ-rejecters stand?

When Jesus had risen from the dead and was about to ascend into heaven, He gave them extensive teaching about the kingdom of God (see Acts 1:3). They asked Him, "Are you at this time going to restore the kingdom to Israel?" (v. 6). That was not only their priority, but also their interpretation of the kingdom of God—i.e., a nationalistic issue. They were interested in times and seasons. Jesus said:

It is not for you to know the times or dates the Father has set by his own authority. But you will receive power when the Holy Spirit comes on you; and you will be my witnesses in Jerusalem, and in all Judea and Samaria, and to the ends of the earth (Acts 1:7,8).

Those were the last words of Jesus on earth. True, not everybody can give up their fishing boats to fish for men. But the Great Commission must still remain the top priority for *all* believers.

Future Evangelism

The world can be evangelized sooner than most believe, even as we begin the new millennium. There were only a few thousand believers when Jesus left this world—perhaps one Christian follower for every 20,000 people. Yet within 300 years the entire Roman Empire became "officially" Christian. Today it is estimated there are more than 600 million born-again Christians on earth. That is 1 in every 10 people.

If we are distracted by other issues and devote our time, money and energy to mere political and social concerns, the gospel witness will decrease. It must increase. We need one final, all-out effort to reach the other nine-tenths of the world. When the gospel has been preached in the entire world as a witness to all the nations, the end will come at last (see Matt. 24:14).

EVANGELISM AND THE WORLD

When considering the scope and ramifications of the Great Commission, one cannot help but be indelibly impressed by the fact that it is an expression of the love of God to the whole world. That is why, whatever his or her career, the Christian's main business is evangelism. Evangelism is an indispensable part of any Christian ministry.

Let There Be Light

When Paul was in Troas, he preached all night. As he preached, a young man called Eutychus drifted off and fell out of a window. Fortunately, Paul was there to restore him to life.

We read: "There were many lamps in the upstairs room where we were meeting" (Acts 20:8). Well, there are many lamps in our world today, too. The virgins in the parable of the bridegroom all had lamps, but half the lamps had gone out (see Matt. 25:8). By the way, that doesn't mean the lamps were half out. We can't be half lit; we either shine or we are a patch of shadow.

I sometimes wonder if 50/50 is a general average among Christians. Half the virgins were asleep. So was Eutychus, and look what happened to him! People who go to sleep on the job, those whose lamps have gone out because they have no oil, are bound to fall. Perhaps that is why we read, "Wake up, O sleeper, rise from the dead, and Christ will shine on you" (Eph. 5:14).

If you want to dispel the darkness, there is no use arguing with it. Just switch the light on! Polemics is no substitute dynamic for truth and the Holy Spirit. No amount of darkness can extinguish the light of a single candle.

Jesus said that John was "the burning and shining lamp" (John 5:35, *NKJV*). In John 1:5,7 (*NKJV*) we read, "The light shines in the darkness." John came "to bear witness of the Light." It strikes me that if the light was already shining, why was John needed? When the sun rises we all know about it; we don't need anybody to testify that it is daylight.

So, what is a "witness" of light? If you look into the sky on most clear nights, the moon is shining. Men have been to the moon and they know it generates no light of its own. Also, all space surrounding the moon is void of light. If space is dark and the moon has no light of its own, why is it so bright and how can it bring light to us? We all know, of course, that the moon only reflects light, and that the light comes from the sun. Well, if the sunlight passes through space to reach the moon, why is space so dark, even in the vicinity of the moon?

The answer is actually very elementary!

Light itself is invisible. *You only know light is present when it strikes an object.* Most of space is completely empty. There is nothing there to catch the light from the sun or impede the light until it reaches the moon. Actually, space is full of light generated by billions of suns, yet it appears pitch-black.

The universe is full of God. He is the Father of lights and all light comes from Him. Yet millions walk around in profound darkness. How can that be? How can people walk in spiritual darkness when the whole universe is steeped in the light of God?

These people cannot see the light of invisible things until somebody else catches the light and reflects it. The sun's rays would not be seen on earth, but they illuminate the molecules of our atmosphere, as well as the dust and moisture in the air. The sun radiates light across billions of miles, and yet there is no trace of it until the light is reflected. We need something to show us it is there. The moon is a witness to the light. It proves that the sun is shining, because it shines with the light of the sun. The moon sails across the sky in invisible sunlight and passes on enough for us to find our way.

First Timothy 1:17 talks about "the King eternal, immortal, invisible." The light of God is constant, brilliant. It is never intermittent. But who sees it? People walk in darkness. The stark fact is that the only light they will ever see is reflected light. Just as John was a "burning and-shining lamp," a witness to the Light, so is every believer. We are commanded to "walk in the light" (1 John 1:7), for if we don't, there will be no light. A spiritually lost world depends upon light reflectors. *If we hide the gospel, it will remain hidden to those who are lost* (see 2 Cor. 4:3-6).

Perhaps I can point something out here. Paul says that the face of Moses shone with the glory of God, but he veiled his face (see 2 Cor. 3:13). The reason he veiled it was not humility, humble as he was. It was because the glory would fade, and he knew it would be a bad thing if the superstitious people of Israel saw the glory disappearing. They would draw wrong conclusions from the diminishing effect. So he veiled his face altogether so that they would not know whether his face was shining or not.

Paul's point is that the light of God, His glory, in the Christian age does not fade (see 2 Cor. 3:18). It is permanent. The veil is taken away because there is no need to fear that it will vanish after a short time. The Spirit of God is not a will-o'-the-wisp, flickering uncertainly around our lives. He abides with us. We can walk openly and unveiled before the world, so that people may see the glory of God in us.

James says, "Every good gift . . . comes down from the Father of lights, with whom there is no variation or shadow of turning" (Jas. 1:17, NKJV). As the NIV puts it, God "does not change like shifting shadows." The sun causes a shadow as it turns and the shadow moves. You see that on a sundial, which is how it keeps time. When there is no shadow, the sun is directly overhead at its zenith. God never casts a shadow at all, because He is always at the zenith. And He never shifts from that perfect position. The light of God is ceaseless, not temporary, and always fully radiant.

His is the everlasting light we are to eternally reflect. Our faces should not be veiled, as His glory will not pass away. We are being changed "from glory to glory" (2 Cor. 3:18, NKJV)—we are given more and more glory!

Will Darkness Fall on America?

Why should I, an evangelist, come to America? Isn't there light here already, more than in India, Egypt or Benin? Well, there is light here. America has the gospel. At almost every street corner, it seems, a church spire points like a finger upward to God. Am I trying to bring light where there is already light?

Remember the story I told of the tribe that worshiped the moon? They thought the sun was stupid to shine during the daytime when there was plenty of light. They failed to consider that there is plenty of light during the day only because the sun is shining.

There is light in the streets of America, but only because there are Christians here who allow their lights to shine. Jesus said, "You are the light of the world" (Matt. 5:14), so I am happy to come and shine with you all. We can always do with more light. Without Christians, night would soon fall on America. Non-Christians would have it the way they wanted, but they would soon reap what they have sowed. Without a guiding light, there would be total anarchy.

Many Americans say they can live decent lives without Christianity. But I wonder. They seem to have forgotten that the very idea of decency in America originated with the nation's Christian forefathers. People can live without breathing, but only briefly. They can live without food and water a bit longer and without light for a while, but not forever.

The spiritual capital invested in America by previous generations of believers will eventually be exhausted. We can't live only on the dividends of their investments. We must be wealth creators—brokers of spiritual wealth, the riches of faith. We would put some of those much-admired Greek philosophers in jail for pedophilia if they were alive today. It was Christ who saved Europe, not Plato. Christ alone can save America. They say the price of freedom is eternal vigilance, but vigilance alone will fail without faith in God. Freedom is a side effect of godliness. You can't have an effect without its cause, and freedom without faith in God leads to slavery.

Many countries I visit have no Christian tradition that shapes their policies. A foundation reinforced with Bible faith is what distinguishes nations—and will extinguish them if abandoned. Something like this happened in my country, Germany.

Centuries of liberal and rationalistic thought and biblical criticism diluted the Christian faith in my homeland. Weak and unstable as water, the region could not excel (see Gen. 49:4). Given these conditions, it was easy for an amoral regime to take over. The barbaric policies of Hitler and the Third Reich met with little resistance.

In the eighteenth century, the experiment of a Christless state brought the Reign of Terror to France, resulting in the slaughter of two million people. Britain was spared from this savagery mainly because of the impact of the Wesley-Whitefield revival movement. It will take at least a generation for Russia to recover from 70 years of imposed atheism.

Worse, perhaps, are the rampant forms of Christianity that have been corrupted and mutilated beyond recognition. They devalue the gospel with unbelieving theories, gross superstition and idolatry. They impart no freedom because they don't offer the truth. This world cries out for full-blooded gospel evangelism.

The Work of an Evangelist

The Great Commission, which comes from the lips of Christ Himself, is found in varying forms in the four Gospels and in the book of Acts. Each time the emphasis is on the nations—the unsaved masses all over the world. In Matthew's Gospel we read, "Go therefore and make disciples of all the nations" (28:19, *NKJV*). Mark says, "Go into all the world and preach the gospel to every creature" (16:15, *NKJV*). John records Jesus' most sacred moment when He spoke to His Father: "As you sent me into the world, I have sent them into the world . . . that the world may believe that you have sent me" (John 17:18,21).

Some people regard an evangelist as a revivalist, that is, someone who gives a church a good rousing shake-up once a year. But an evangelist's job is to win people for Christ, not to preach to sleeping Christians and revive dead churches! An evangelistic campaign is not to be confused with a church jamboree. An evangelist's ministry is misdirected if it is aimed at the saints of God. The gift of evangelism is given for him to make contact with unconverted men and women for Christ.

Evangelism Is for All Christians

The New Testament makes it clear that evangelism is the natural function of all who follow Christ. In fact, evangelism *is* following Christ, for that is what He mainly did. Faith and its propagation are two sides of the same coin. A believer has no option; he must be engaged in telling others about his faith, or in some way be involved in that business.

All religions have their sacred obligations. Sikhs must wear a turban. Hindus must avoid animal fats. Muslims repeat their sacred prayer. Christians have a sacred obligation to witness for Christ. Witnessing is the business of the Christian faith. The Church is the society for the propagation of the gospel. In its first-century beginnings, people joined the Church expecting to be witnesses, even though the risks were high.

Even before his conversion, Paul knew that telling others about Christ is what a believer must do, and he persecuted the Church for doing its sacred duty. After his conversion, Paul himself got into a great deal of trouble for sharing his faith. Yet as an apostle he displayed a very forgivable and natural pride that God had entrusted him with the gospel. He always spoke as if it was the most unexpected good fortune.

The Church is supposed to grow in numbers. That is implicit throughout the New Testament. It is also explicit:

How shall they preach unless they are sent? As it is written: How beautiful are the feet of those who preach the gospel of peace, who bring glad tidings of good things (Rom. 10:15, *NKJV*).

The World in Our Sights

One striking difference between the Hebrew and Christian Scriptures is that the New Testament brings *the world* into focus. The Old Testament is confined largely to Israel's disappointing history. The highest hopes of God's people were strictly nationalistic, their outlook merely an "in-look." In the New Testament the whole picture changes.

Suddenly there is bustle and excitement. After Christ commissions them to spread the gospel, the men of Israel become world travelers, proclaiming the name of the Lord everywhere. Jesus tells them in John 10:16, "Other sheep I have which are not of this fold; them also I must bring" (*NKJV*).

When He spoke of His mission and that of His Church, Jesus talked about shepherding and harvesting, but He also talked about fishing. One day, while taking a walk along the edge of the water, He watched several young Galilean fishermen at work. Simon and Andrew were there casting a net, while nearby John and James were mending their nets. Some were little more than teenagers. Jesus said to them, "Follow me, and I will make you fishers of men" (Matt. 4:19). Whether they are more like sheep or fish is not important—Christ wanted to gather people to Himself. That is still His great purpose, and it should be ours, too.

Fishing in the Sea

What fishing and the sea meant to Israel should be better understood. The Israelites were never enthusiastic about the sea. They didn't fish in the Mediterranean, but rather in the tiny sea of Galilee. Israel did not have its own shipping fleets; they used the ships of Tarshish with foreign crews, like the ship Jonah boarded at Joppa.

The Old Testament does mention the sea but rarely depicts it in a favorable light. To the Jewish people, the sea was the mysterious deep, the place of creeping things and the Leviathan (see Ps. 104:25,26), a snakelike creature, bending and twisting. Isaiah 27:1 depicts the Leviathan as a crooked serpent, the dragon that is in the sea. Psalm 74 speaks of the dragons and the Leviathan in the waters. A sea monster swallowed Jonah. Near the end of his revelation, John heaves a sigh of relief and says, "There was no more sea" (Rev. 21:1, *NKJV*).

The sea was a wild and treacherous element considered to be beyond human control. Only God could tame the sea. Psalm 104:6 reads: "You covered [the earth] with the deep as with a garment; the waters stood above the mountains. But at your rebuke the waters fled." He opened a path through the Red Sea for the Israelites, but at His command the sea destroyed the Egyptian army.

The psalmist spoke of "the stormy wind, which lifts up the waves of the sea. They mount up to the heavens, they go down again to the depths" (Ps. 107:25,26, *NKJV*). In this passage, the sailors "reel to and fro, and stagger like a drunken man, and are at their wits' end" (v. 27).

The sea was thought to be a place of the dead, home to howling and haunting spirits. Revelation 20:13 reads: "The sea gave up the dead." The dismal wind shrieked like lost souls in torment. When the disciples saw Jesus walking on the sea, they thought He was a ghost and they were terrified (see Matt. 14:26).

This dread of the deep also found expression as a picture of the nations:

Woe to the multitude of many people who make a noise like the roar of the seas, and to the rushing of nations that make a rushing like the rushing of mighty waters! The nations will rush like the rushing of many waters (Isa. 17:12,13, *NKJV*).

Psalm 2:1 speaks of the nations raging. Jesus described the nations in similar terms in Luke 21:25: "On the earth distress of nations, with perplexity, the sea and the waves roaring; men's hearts failing them from fear" (*NKJV*).

And yet despite the dangers, Jesus called His disciples to be fishermen. He said, "I will make you fishers of men" (Matt. 4:19), not merely in Galilee, but "to the ends of the earth" (Acts 1:8). To the sea of humanity. To all nations. These Galileans knew little of the world. They had never moved far from their little fishing town. They were not adventurers, but Christ was sending them on the greatest adventure ever undertaken by people. They would fish for men and women for Christ in the wild waters of the world. That is where they would catch them. This was deep-sea fishing, where tempests rage, where devils are let loose. The waters of adversity would threaten them.

When Jesus called them He showed them that He was master of the seas. They were professional fishermen; but Jesus took over as the new managing executive of Zebedee & Sons, commandeered one of their boats and told the fishermen how to do their job. The result? He produced a harvest of the sea such as they had never even dreamed about (see Luke 5:1-11).

One day the disciples were inching their way across the Sea of Galilee, held in the teeth of an unrelenting storm. They could do nothing but wait it out and pray for salvation. Then they saw Jesus walking on the sea in one of the greatest of all acted parables. The elements were at their worst, the very devil having whipped up the lake's fury, yet Jesus calmly walked the waves. He did not fear the dragon of the deep. The shrieking winds and the devil gave Him no pause; He was their Master and trod them underfoot. He rebuked their raging and they sank back like whipped dogs and, with a whimper, lay quiet beneath His feet (see Matt. 14:22-33).

Jesus warned His disciples that He was sending them out into wild waters to teach all nations. People would kill them, thinking they were doing God a service (see John 16:2). They would be like sheep in the midst of wolves (see Matt. 10:16). They had to be prepared to lay down their lives. They knew nothing of the wisdom of Greece, of the far-flung empire of Rome, or what lay beyond the Pillars of Hercules. The world was an unknown ocean full of possible dangers. *But Christ had demonstrated that He was Master of heaven and earth, the sea and the dry land. Wherever they went He was Lord.*

WHEN JESUS SENT US INTO THE WORLD TO MAKE DISCIPLES OF ALL THE NATIONS, HE HAD ONLY SUCCESS IN MIND.

They went as He said, fishing stormy waters at His direction. They mocked the howling devils of persecution and defied the winds of adversity. They let down their nets at His command and out of the restless turbulence of mankind they made their catches and filled their boat.

What does all this mean for us today?

The world today is not less troubled, nor less dangerous. Yet the gospel is advancing on all fronts. Like an incoming tide, filling up the little creeks and crannies, the Christian faith is flooding the devil's territories. When Jesus sent us, His servants, into all nations, He had only success in mind. Twice He ordered the disciples to cast their nets (see Luke 5:1-11 and John 21:1-14). The first time was *before* His resurrection and the second time was *after*. The second time the catch was greater than the first time, and the nets did not break then, either. This was prophetic.

The early disciples swept the seas with their nets, but we are now nearing the end of time. Across the world we see 50 times more people won for Christ each day than on the Day of Pentecost. At a crusade in Liberia, in one meeting, we saw 150,000 souls respond to the call of salvation.

What About Methodology?

The account of Paul's meeting with King Agrippa, grandson of Herod the Great, is found in the book of Acts, chapters 25 and 26. Face to face with this powerful ruler, Paul was not afraid to stand up for what he believed. He said to King Agrippa, "I have had God's help to this very day, and so I stand here and testify to small and great alike" (Acts 26:22). Paul did not debate methods. He spoke of Christ, whenever and wherever he could—in synagogues, on riverbanks, in the open-air schools of the philosophers, in private rooms, before great crowds, at the Acropolis, by the river, aboard ships. He even witnessed to a suicidal jailer in the middle of an earthquake.

Various strong opinions abound in the Church about how to reach men and women for Christ. Some insist that this is purely the initiative of God. He suddenly enters the field, visits an area, saves those He has chosen and then leaves. Then the field lies dormant until another crop is ready for election.

Charles Finney taught that revivals happen as and when we follow the rules of revival. Later, campaigns were considered to be the most effective technique. Others watch and offer their criticism, opposed to all structured efforts. They say that one-to-one witnessing alone is worthwhile. Fruit must be handpicked, they say. These and other methods and means—art, music, literature, youth work, street work and so on—all have their advocates.

In fact, the analysis of evangelistic methods has become quite a science. We study the rules of success, the best business practices, the psychology of communication and advertising, learn how to broadcast and make an impression on television. Well, perhaps God appreciates our efforts to do the job properly. I only wonder whether all our seminars and studies can equal the simple enthusiasm such as Paul displayed when he spoke to small and great as the opportunity arose. His answer as to which is the best way is this: "That I might by all means save some" (1 Cor. 9:22, *NKJV*).

The means must match the moment. *People talk about jumping at the opportunity, but I think Paul kept jumping until opportunity came.* I preach to very large congregations of unconverted people. I believe that is the way for me, but in our campaigns we try to utilize every ministry and every talent. We walk with our feet, see with our eyes and work with our hands. The best method is when we each do what we do best, using our own specific methods and not imitating others. But, believe me, somebody will be saved by our peculiar approach who would otherwise never be reached.

Whitefield in the U.S.A.

Think of America. In the beginning, a fine foundation was laid. That is still very evident. Some 100 years after the pilgrim fathers first set foot in what is now the United States, one man had a particular role to play in the founding of the nation. He was not a politician, but an evangelist: George Whitefield.

Whitefield was born and preached his first sermon in Gloucester, England, a city 2,000 years old. He made seven evangelistic tours in America and died during his last trip in 1770. The last time anyone saw him alive, he was preaching with a flickering candle in his hand to a crowd of friends. The Whitefield Memorial Church in Gloucester has a stone portico engraved with the words of Whitefield: "The love of Christ constrains me to lift up my voice like a trumpet."

Also, facing the church is a statue of Robert Raikes, who came from the same city. He opened the world's first Sunday School in 1780. He had seen children in the street, like heathens, playing in the shadow of the great 1,400-year-old cathedral. He taught his ragged schoolchildren in a little cottage nearby. This all took place not so very far from Plymouth, where the pilgrim fathers boarded the Mayflower for their historic voyage to America.

Outlook: The Nations

The biblical outlook on evangelism is not just for individuals but entire nations. The Old Testament prophets did not run missions in backstreet hired halls and advertise their prophetic ministry. They spoke to kings and rulers to influence their policies. Elijah appeared before Ahab and took over the weather bureau for three years (see 1 Kings 17:1; 18:1). Jonah shook up the most powerful city on earth with his preaching, causing its king to tremble upon his throne (see Jon. 3:6). Daniel's visions of the future foretold the fate of empires (see Dan. 9—11).

Later in the early days of the Church, nothing was done in a corner. Jesus Himself was a public figure whom the leaders of the nation had to reckon with. But even after his death, the apostles did not slip away into comfortable little nests and run village churches and garden clubs, leaning over the garden gate and chewing a straw. They endured the animosity of howling mobs to confront the highest ranks in the cities. When Paul went anywhere, his enemies had only to follow the uproar to locate him. Yet God arranged for him to go before kings and rulers and even the Roman emperor. Since then, throughout history, governments and rulers have not been able to ignore the Church.

We must see the gospel in the highest terms. While the gospel is a radical new order for the city, it is nothing less than a nation saver. This is not a pleasant, Sunday-afternoon religion with a sprinkle of spirituality, a bit of psychology to help us along. We do not provide prayer as a generic tranquilizer, sprinkling sugar in the bitter black-coffee cup of life. We do not promote a pray-and-feel-calmer brand of meditation or hold classes in spiritual aerobics. Church is not just a place for "the old to close their eyes and the young to eye their clothes." *It is a power pack for the nations, designed to put a dynamic charge into all life.*

New Age philosophy has simply nothing to offer compared with the gospel. Candles may as well try to outshine the sun! The gospel is for the whole man and the whole world. The gospel is not just a road map left by the side of the road to help lonely pilgrims find their own way to heaven; it provides a solid rock foundation for our lives. (Why has the Lord left 600 million born-again people on earth instead of rapturing them all to glory? Because God deals through individuals and that 600 million could win 600 million friends this year.)

God is not a mini-God. He is the God of heaven and earth, kings and kingdoms, presidents and republics. He presides over the eternal destiny of us all. That does not mean the ministry should address only parliaments or work for changes in legislation. A church is not a local chapter of the Republican or Democratic party. That is work for Christian politicians, not for those called to declare the unsearchable riches of Christ. The apostolic commission is to reach the lost of this world, not to address environmental projects, wildlife issues or social engineering.

The era of mass evangelism was thought to have passed by the time of the last world war. In fact, true mass evangelism had never been known and was only just beginning with the rallies of Billy Graham. In 1949, a gospel campaign in Argentina drew 400,000 to one meeting and from it 148 churches came into existence.

Jesus promised, "Anyone who has faith in me will do even greater things than I have done" (see John 14:12). That had nothing to do with healings or miracles of nature, but with the real work of God—salvation. Now we are seeing Christ's word fulfilled.

Revival Teaching

The subject of revival is on the minds of many Christians today. There are certain events which we call "revival." This is a human assessment. By revival, we usually mean events that are superior and distinct from the normal work of the Holy Spirit. We ourselves decide which events are revival and which are not, as the Bible gives us no criteria whatever for making such a distinction. In fact, the Bible says nothing about any work of the Spirit being unique. We devise our own measuring rods for this purpose.

Many try to define revival as if it were a biblical word, but it is not. We identify an event or series of events as a revival and then try to define the word. If we don't know what we mean by revival, how can we can define what is and what is not revival? We should know what we are talking about.

The basic question is, does God have two levels of spiritual action? The ordinary work of the Spirit goes on all the time everywhere. But is there another kind, a super, special power that is in operation when God *really* goes to town? Can we accept two categories of Holy Spirit activity—full power and half power?

Frankly, I don't intend to answer these questions. I merely raise the issue to point out a potential danger: that many are waiting for God to act, for God to enter the field. Whatever our thoughts on revival, the clear teaching of Jesus is to preach the gospel to every creature. There is no salvation apart from it. "It pleased God by the foolishness of preaching to save them that shall believe" (1 Cor. 1:21, *KJV*).

Many insist that an evangelistic campaign is not a revival. OK, don't call it a revival. Call it what it is: a campaign. It doesn't matter what we call it, as long as souls are being delivered from Satan and sin (see Acts 26:18). We should not despise what is being done. On the other hand, people are often heard praying, "Lord, do it again!" They want God to repeat an event they have in mind as a role model. They want an *encore*. But does God *give* encores, no matter how much we applaud His past performances?

If revival is meant for the growth of the Church, what we see today is something never known before in all of history. I have been blessed with the privilege of preaching to a half-million people and seeing with my own eyes hundreds of thousands converted in one service. Modern Church experience and growth has eclipsed those recorded in the Acts of the Apostles a thousand-fold. Take a look at China, where Christians expect to suffer for their faith. When Chairman Mao Tse-tung took over in China, there were a million Christians. Since his death in 1976, there has been an expansion of the faith and the latest estimates run as high as 120 million Chinese Christians, despite continued restriction and government threats.

Much of what is happening does not meet any classical theological formula for conversions or for revival. People who love Jesus and die for Him, as they have done in countless numbers, cannot be inferior believers. When I see tens of thousands clamoring to receive Christ in an open field in Africa or a stadium in India, rejoicing in their experience, I look around for any other kind of "revival" and see none. Can we brush this aside contemptuously as not qualifying as revival because it does not correspond to some eighteenth- or nineteenth-century model?

I believe that world revival is taking place. It has been prayed for long enough. Hymns have asked for it. And now it is on the way. In Korea, a Buddhist country, 40 percent of the population are born-again Christians, including a third of the armed forces. But how does this come about? By evangelism—of every kind.

There has never been a true revival without the preaching of the gospel. It has been said millions of times that prayer precedes revival. Of course it does. It is bound to do so because people pray all the time, so when revival comes it can easily be said to have been produced by prayer. But examination of the records reveals that the major impetus all historic revivals had in common was evangelism! When people went forward and preached the gospel, even in the darkest and most unlikely times, God honored His Word. Extraordinary numbers of people came to Christ, often because extraordinary numbers of people were hearing the Word for the first time.

Revival may come *through* a revived church or *to* a dead church. The Spirit of the Lord has absolute freedom of movement in this world, and He works in myriad ways. Let us set our sails to catch any breeze from God that blows, whatever our particular views about revival. If anyone believes that revival will come, fine. But meanwhile, God can save multitudes of souls. A repeat performance of the awakenings of the past would be great, but *events today are bringing in far more people to salvation than anything ever known*. Indeed, doing our part, doing what we can, may prove to be the catalyst that brings about the very revival many are waiting for.

LEARNING FROM THE MASTER

As we consider such important subjects as revival and evangelism, we have a lot to learn from Jesus Himself. Some of the best-known texts used for gospel preaching come from the teachings of Christ and are found in John's Gospel. Many people have known them since childhood and usually, at least for the older ones among us, in the *King James Version.* Following are famous verses from the book of John. They are like great music of which you never tire. Just relax with God's Word! Let's indulge ourselves with some of the most wonderful words ever written.

> As many as received him, to them gave he power to become the sons of God, even to them that believe on his name (John 1:12).

> Behold the Lamb of God, which taketh away the sin of the world (John 1:29).

Verily, verily, I say unto thee, except a man be born of water and of the Spirit, he cannot enter into the kingdom of God (John 3:5).

For God so loved the world, that he gave his only begotten Son, that whosoever believeth in him should not perish, but have everlasting life (John 3:16).

He that believeth on him is not condemned: but he that believeth not is condemned already, because he hath not believed in the name of the only begotten Son of God (John 3:18).

Whosoever drinketh of the water that I shall give him shall never thirst; but the water that I shall give him shall be in him a well of water springing up into everlasting life (John 4:14).

[We] know that this is indeed the Christ, the Savior of the world (John 4:42).

I am the living bread which came down from heaven: if any man eat of this bread, he shall live for ever: and the bread that I will give is my flesh, which I will give for the life of the world (John 6:51).

I am the light of the world: he that followeth me shall not walk in darkness, but shall have the light of life. If ye believe not that I am he, ye shall die in your sins (John 8:12,24).

Ye shall know the truth and the truth shall make you free. If the Son therefore shall make you free, ye shall be free indeed (John 8:32,36).

I am the door: by me if any man enter in, he shall be saved, and shall go in and out, and find pasture. I am the good shepherd: the good shepherd giveth his life for the sheep (John 10:9,11).

These are treasures, gems in the jewel box of the Gospel of John. There is simply nothing like the Word of God by which to learn how to save the world. Whatever I could say from experience, I will tell you this: One chapter of John's Gospel alone is as powerful and stimulating as the experience of any evangelist. This is the *original* source of all inspiration, the Word of God.

So, for what follows, I go to the source of all resources. Like the householder Jesus described in Matthew 13:52, I want to share treasures old and new.

John the Baptist

I think it would be fair to say that more sermons are prepared on chapter 3 of the book of John than any other. An important section of this text deals with John the Baptist, the first evangelist in the New Testament. John is named 19 times in this Gospel.

John had one single aim: to bring Israel back to God. His ministry was to the whole nation. The idea of individual conversion is not emphasized in the Old Testament and John was the last of the Old Testament prophets. John addressed the Pharisees as a group, but he gave them no hope, even of repentance. He had to baptize people as individuals, but that was simply part of the wholesale work of turning the entire country Godward, fulfilling the prophecy of Malachi (see Mal. 4:5,6).

Christ "is the Savior of all men, especially of those who believe" (1 Tim. 4:10, *NKJV*). That was the basic message of John the Baptist. He called for Israel to start again, to be reborn as a nation. Israel needed to recover its lost spiritual status before God. Isaiah had already said what the Baptist was saying: "Look to the rock from which you were cut and to the quarry from which you were hewn; look to Abraham, your father. . . . When I called him . . . I blessed him" (Isa. 51:1,2).

John preached, "Repent, for the kingdom of heaven is near" (Matt. 3:2). That was the Baptist's hope for Israel—to be the kingdom of God. He spoke of the great One who was to come, and he expected the promised Messiah to lead the nation to victory. They would have to prepare for His coming and be fit to receive Him.

Israel had declined since the days of its pristine glory. Everyone trusted in his or her national identity. If you belonged to Israel you were safe. The Israelites all supposed they had favored-nation status with God, as if God were theirs by birthright. This belief comes through in Psalm 87:5,6: "And of Zion it will be said, 'This one and that one were born in her. . . .' The LORD will record, when He registers the peoples: 'This one was born there'" (NKJV). It's as if proof of residence were your passport to heaven. You were a national of the kingdom of God, and the rest had to go through immigration.

John the Baptist dealt with this very issue. He said, "Do not think you can say to yourselves, 'We have Abraham as our father.' I tell you that out of these stones God can raise up children for Abraham" (Matt. 3:9). The ax was laid to the root of the tree, and that meant the nation, the ancestral tree. They boasted of being the children of their fathers and of Israel; but Israel could be cut off. John's message, therefore, was: "Repent." Malachi had said that Elijah would return and "turn the heart of the fathers to the children, and the heart of the children to their fathers, lest I come and smite the earth with a curse" (4:6, KJV). John the Baptist's role was that of Elijah.

John wanted Israel to begin again, so he tried to take them back to square one. They would be required to start where Israel had begun with Moses. First, the people had to come to John in the wilderness. He never preached in any city. Second, they had to pass through the waters, just as Moses had led Israel through the Red Sea. He baptized a representative part of the nation in Jordan. By passing through the waters, the nation could be reborn. Third, the children of Israel had to recapture their spiritual position, which called for *repentance*.

Now, before I go any further, let me make this comment about the Church today. Repentance must be a powerful element in our gospel message. John the Baptist made no bones about it—the people would either repent or there was national disaster ahead. John was the evangelist extraordinaire. He was the prototype of all that an evangelist should be: fearless, uncompromising with sin, declaring the righteousness and judgment of God. In fact, Jesus Himself began His ministry repeating the message of John, saying "Repent, for the kingdom of heaven is near" (Matt. 4:17).

The Church is often accused of not providing moral leadership in the land. I wonder if the preaching of righteousness and judgment is anything like the dominant note it should be. Has the gospel been reduced to a promise of sugar and spice and everything nice? God promised Israel a land flowing with milk and honey, but the Law was placed at the very heart of the nation. The Church *must* proclaim the contrast between godliness and ungodliness, right and wrong, truth and untruth, good and evil. In fact, the world expects it.

John the Baptist and Nicodemus

Nearly half of the third chapter of John is about John the Baptist. But we must link John the Baptist with the man who came to Jesus by night: Nicodemus. Nicodemus had heard John's message. He almost certainly believed that John was a prophet and that Israel needed to turn from their sin if they were to see the nation raised up again to be powerful and independent.

But John worked no miracles and Jesus did. Nicodemus *knew* God was with Jesus, that He was a teacher who had come from God. So he went to Jesus in search of understanding about Israel and the Kingdom. Nicodemus was one of the chief teachers of Israel and sought the truth for his nation.

Jesus brought Nicodemus face-to-face with reality. John taught that the nation must be reborn by passing through the waters, just as Israel had originally come into national existence by passing through the Red Sea and the Jordan River. But Jesus said that the rebirth of the nation required more than a physical undertaking. He said, "No one can enter the kingdom of God unless he is born of water *and* the Spirit" (John 3:5, emphasis mine).

Jesus spoke to Nicodemus not only as an individual but also as a teacher of Israel. When He spoke of being born again, Jesus did not use the word "you" in the singular. The message of rebirth is not only for individuals but for whole nations. A nation can be reborn by the preaching of the gospel. John 3:16 (*KJV*) says, "God so loved *the world*," and then *"whosoever." The gospel is for the whole world*. That is what we are aiming for in Africa—a blood-washed continent. Africa has a choice: either be washed in the blood of tribal conflict or washed in the redeeming blood of Jesus.

Prophets: God's Mouthpieces

John proclaimed the word of the Lord to the people of God, Israel. Elijah spoke to Israel—one man preaching to every tribe! What Elijah or any other prophet was, the Church is today. We are to speak out to a whole nation. The ministry of the church is *prophetic*. Some people claim to have a prophetic ministry, as if they were different from other Christians. In fact, the whole of God's people has now received the Spirit of prophecy, the Holy Spirit. *The gospel is prophetic.*

Jesus confirmed this. He said, "Among those born of women there has not risen one greater than John the Baptist; but he who is least in the kingdom of heaven is greater than he" (Matt. 11:11, *NKJV*). Those who are born of the Spirit and are in the kingdom of God today are greater in this sense than John, because we have the great prophetic truth of the gospel.

That is our calling, our responsibility. *Prophets must prophesy. Witnesses must witness.* Paul said, "Woe is me if I do not preach the gospel" (1 Cor. 9:16, *NKJV*). Jeremiah tried not to prophesy, but he found that God's word was like a fire burning in his bones (see Jer. 20:9). We dare not be like Jonah and go to sleep while everybody around us is in danger.

Fire: God's Means

Preaching salvation must be more than a cold-water business. Conversions come in the fire. Evangelism is not a clinical operation; it is a hot affair. Conversion must be of the Spirit. This is not a business transaction. Holy Spirit preaching makes Holy Spirit converts, not technical converts or theological converts. With the heart we believe. The answer for this nation is not polemics and debate, but the consistent, bright-burning witness of genuine believers. Let me remind you, if you want to be rid of the darkness, stop arguing and just switch the light on!

In John 4, Jesus went outside Israel to Samaria. He ignored all protocol and social taboos and directly addressed a woman— a foreign woman! Worse still, He asked her for a drink from her own vessel, which was considered defiled. She was a Samaritan, a people particularly loathed by the Jews. Astonished at Christ's breach of all social etiquette, she talked to Him and Christ exposed her sinful life. He knew she was just about the worst woman in town, but He gave to her the water of life. She came to the well for water carrying a water pot. When He sent her away, she left the water pot and took the well with her—the well of life. He revealed His identity to her when He had not revealed Himself to any other Gentile until that time.

There are more details to be considered here. Jesus had told the woman to go and bring her husband. She went off and whether the man she was living with came or not I don't know, but she brought everybody else's husband with her! She had returned to her village, saying, "Come, see a man." This woman was well known for her "men"; she had been crazy about half a dozen men and now here was number seven (bringing to mind what the Sadducees once asked Jesus [see Matt. 22:23-28] about seven husbands and one wife—whose wife would she be in heaven?). Yet nobody else in that town could have done the job so well. "Come, see a man," she said, and they came.

Well, you may have read that at that time the men's robes were white. So Jesus lifted up His eyes and saw this white-clad crowd coming to see Him, and He said to His disciples, "Lift up your eyes and look at the fields, for they are already white for harvest!" (John 4:35, *NKJV*). This woman was already bringing in the sheaves.

Now take a look at verses 31-34:

Meanwhile his disciples urged him, "Rabbi, eat something."

But he said to them, "I have food to eat that you know nothing about."

Then his disciples said to each other, "Could someone have brought him food?"

"My food," said Jesus, "is to do the will of him who
sent me and to finish his work."

What was that work which gave to Christ more satisfaction
than a meal to a hungry man? Evangelism. Whenever Jesus
talked about His own satisfaction or joy, His pleasure arose from
doing God's will. It was never just a sudden emotion coming
over Him, but it always came out of some critical moment when
He had successfully negotiated a stage in God's plan.

The disciple is not above His Lord. If we want the joy of
Christ, we must do what Christ did. For Him, satisfaction was
not the result of finding some Christian pleasure to compete
with the world's pleasure. It was not a question of being enter-
tained by church performances instead of secular performances.
Christ does not compete by promising a religious equivalent of
what the world offers, pleasure for pleasure. It is completely different. *The pleasure of Christ is the will of God and its enactment.* No
dance, no concert, no sensational movie can compete with winning a soul for Christ.

"Do you not say, 'Four months more and then the harvest'?"
(v. 35). Well, His disciples did say that. It was an aphorism, like
our saying, "Rome wasn't built in a day." But the harvest He
spoke of was the harvest that was there before their eyes, represented in the sheaves this woman had herself reaped. But Israel
had a tendency to expect the work of God to take place tomorrow—tomorrow the Kingdom would come; tomorrow the
Samaritans would repent; tomorrow the Romans would leave;
tomorrow God would appear again in power like He did in the
Exodus and at Sinai. They had a God for all their yesterdays and
for all their tomorrows, but nothing for today.

That attitude is not unknown in modern times. Smith Wigglesworth once said, "It is not theology we want. It is NOW-ology." We talk about sowing, but little about reaping. Jesus said the fields are ripe for harvest. There is not the slightest doubt that there have been times in the past when vast harvests could have been reaped but were not. The harvest was left to only a few reapers—usually professional preachers or big-time evangelists.

At times, however, the possibilities were seen. The half century following the death of John Wesley saw a far greater extension of the Methodist revival in England than during his lifetime.

General William Booth said that in the late Victorian period, anybody could stand at any street corner at any time and preach the gospel and a crowd would gather to listen. Yet one of the best-known evangelists in Britain tried to stop others from conducting crusades because it would detract from his own success. He offered excellent evangelists large churches if they would cease evangelizing. He mistakenly thought the harvest would last forever. But the lament in Jeremiah 8:20 is, "The harvest is past, the summer has ended, and we are not saved." It is always time to go, so go NOW!

Paul's Declaration

The tremendous sixth chapter of 2 Corinthians is perhaps the greatest chapter ever written on evangelism. Here are searing, challenging words from the heart of the apostle Paul, the man who made the first gospel penetration into Europe. I wish there were space here to repeat it word for word:

> In great endurance; in troubles, hardships, and distress-
> es; in beatings, imprisonments and riots; in hard work,
> sleepless nights and hunger; in purity, understanding,

patience and kindness; in the Holy Spirit . . . through glory and dishonor . . . poor, yet making many rich (2 Cor. 6:4-10).

Consider the way he begins the chapter:

As God's fellow workers we urge you not to receive God's grace in vain. For he says, "In the time of my favor I heard you." Now is the day of salvation. We put no stumbling block in anyone's path, so that our ministry will not be discredited (2 Cor. 6:1-3).

Frankly, though I am neither a scholar nor a Greek expert, I think that in translating the words of Paul in his day into the English of our day, we can miss the passion there. His feelings, his background are not ours, even when we get the words right. As an evangelist, maybe I get just a glimpse of what it really meant.

Paul is overflowing with the wonder of divine grace. He had received grace and he never got over it. The gift of God's grace was so great that it imposed upon him an obligation to share it. He recognized that obligation. Paul knew he was spiritually wealthy beyond the dreams of every religious practitioner who had ever walked the earth. The worst thing he could think of was not sharing it. To do so would be "to receive the grace of God in vain" (2 Cor. 6:1, NKJV).

It was all right to receive that grace. The Corinthians had. They knew it and Paul knew it. It worked for them. But to keep it to themselves meant it all ran into the sand. At all costs, by all means—never mind what suffering—with the utmost energy, endurance and resourcefulness to the limits of our power, people must be told.

Paul said, "Christ's love compels us," because he was convinced that if Christ died for us all then we're all dead (2 Cor. 5:14).

The vital message was: Today is the day of salvation.

Preparing the Ground

Jesus said to His disciples, "I sent you to reap what you have not worked for. Others have done the hard work, and you have reaped the benefits of their labor" (John 4:38). I think John is giving Christ's original words a slightly anticipatory emphasis. Up to that point, the disciples had not labored at all. But the principle remains, nonetheless: *Today's evangelism makes tomorrow's evangelism possible.*

Today, intellectualism is in vogue. Pride—being too clever for this "God stuff"—is the downfall of our civilization. The intellectuals are confused. Those who follow this fad must be taken along by the hand and led toward faith in Christ, with gentleness and wisdom. But, for the most part, we must learn to appreciate the immense power of the gospel when it is preached in its original, unadulterated and passionate form. The gospel has a strange and peculiar power. It finds an opening and reaches a person's heart obliquely. Any mere cleverness or modern psychology on our part is crude in comparison. The ability to understand and manipulate crowd psychology can achieve nothing next to the power of the gospel.

As I mentioned in a previous book, we have been to places where pioneers like David Livingstone and C. T. Studd had worked. Livingstone said that where he had seen little fruit, others would come along with more gospel light and see thousands come to Christ. It was one of the highlights of my life to minister in Blantyre in Malawi, named after the little Scottish town where Livingstone was born. Livingstone labored for

Christ and died in his efforts with little to show for them. But he made it possible for others to succeed, and I was one of them. In Blantyre, we saw 150,000 people turn to Christ—in one week!

My prayer is that I might labor in an acceptable way, just as Paul lays out in 2 Corinthians 6, so that any who follow me shall find the ground less hard. It struck me one day that in the parable of the sower in Matthew 13, some of the seed fell by the wayside and the birds came and ate it. What wayside was this? The sower had made it himself as he walked up and down! He was hardening his own field as he sowed and worked. I thought, *God help me not to make the way harder for others by the way I do what I have to do.*

THE JOY OF HARVEST—THAT IS THE REAL JOY!

Well, Jesus also prepared the ground for others. A few years after the resurrection, another evangelist, Philip, went to Samaria and found the place open and ready for the gospel. There was great joy in that place. Jesus had worked no miracles when He was there—at least the Bible doesn't say He did. But many healing wonders took place and demons were expelled when Philip went to Samaria in the Lord's footsteps. Jesus was a good worker to follow. He could say "Follow me and I will make you fishers of men" without ruining the fishing grounds.

But Jesus also said, "Even now the reaper draws his wages, even now he harvests the crop for eternal life" (John 4:36). The joy of harvest—that is the real joy. Suddenly that old hymn becomes meaningful:

Trust and obey,
For there's no other way
To be happy in Jesus,
But to trust and obey.

I only know two persisting obligations in which Christ calls us to trust and obey: love and evangelism. Your wages are in the work, and you can't enjoy the wages unless you work.

The Obligation of Jesus

Let us look again at this account of Jesus in Samaria. The situation is summed up in verse 4 of John 4: "Now he had to go through Samaria." The *King James Version* reads, "He must needs go through Samaria," and the *New King James Version* reads, "He needed to go through Samaria." But the closest rendering of the Greek is probably found in *The Amplified Bible*: "It was necessary for Him to go through Samaria."

The Greek uses an impersonal verb, *dei*, which is used 105 times in the New Testament. Only once does it mean a physical necessity. In all other cases a moral or emotional necessity is implied. Each time the text indicates the Lord's sense of what He had to do, an obligation—the very purpose of His being on earth rather than a mere physical necessity. We read, for example:

"The Son of Man must suffer many things" (Mark 8:31).

"I must preach the good news of the kingdom of God" (Luke 4:43).

"I must work the works of Him who sent Me" (John 9:4, *NKJV*).

"The Son of Man must be lifted up" (John 12:34).

"He must rise again from the dead" (John 20:9, *NKJV*).

For Jesus, the work of saving men and women was no more to be ignored than the fact that He was one with God. This work was His very *being*. Not only did He save; He *was* salvation. As fire is to heat, so Christ is to salvation. Evangelism was for Him the true categorical imperative.

Jesus said that His "food" was to do the will of God. He later said that He had sent His disciples to do the things He had done:

> As You sent Me into the world, I also have sent them into the world (John 17:18, *NKJV*).

> As the Father has sent Me, I also send you (John 20:21, *NKJV*).

John does not set out the obligation of evangelism in quite the same way as the synoptic Gospels, but it is nonetheless present throughout the book of John, both latent and potent.

The Obligation of the Disciples

Disciples are sent into the world—a world that was, and still is, hostile and unregenerate. The Church today must concern itself not merely with "church growth," which can mean something akin to business growth by wooing other people's customers. Somebody said that we are called to be fishers of men, not keepers of aquariums, pinching fish from other people's aquariums.

The Church in America has a huge religious pool in which to fish. In Europe there is no such religious pool and few potential converts. Not only has Europe become extremely secularized, but part of the tradition of those countries is to be completely free from any religious claim. To win one soul, churches have had to be extremely resourceful and enterprising. Leaders work extremely hard, going all out, and most of the seed seems to fall on infertile ground.

I was told that America is a society composed of two main groups, the religious and the nonreligious, and it is very hard for the religious group to make a real invasion of the other group. Perhaps I am misinformed. I certainly hope so. However, some people consider it a waste of time to reach out to the world of the godless. Yet when I look at the stories emerging from America, I don't think it is impossible. Even now, God is raising spiritual Lazaruses from the dead.

However hard it may or may not be, to reach out to the godless is our task. If American churches are merely family churches, continuing their existence from parents to children and getting by on membership switching, then we had better declare a state of emergency. There has to be a council of war—full-scale war. Desperately needed is a call back to our primary purpose of evangelizing the lost. We are sent into the *world*, not just the Christian realm. We are fishers of men, not just feeders of sheep. We are here to save the nation, not half the nation.

The outside world is a dangerous place, a place of confessors and martyrs. The opposition is not just intellectual but is sometimes armed with guns, knives and stones, as I have seen. The question is, will that world of slaughter overcome the world of the love of Jesus? And are we prepared to let it?

Disappointment Can Be Overcome

Disappointments will come, but they must not be allowed to stop us. Let's go back to John 2:23-25 and read on into 3:2, ignoring the chapter break. The text reads like this:

In Jerusalem . . . many people saw the miraculous signs he was doing and believed in his name. But Jesus would not entrust himself to them, for he knew all men. He did not need man's testimony about man, for he knew what was in a man. Now there was a man of the Pharisees named Nicodemus, a member of the Jewish ruling council. He came to Jesus at night.

Some people are shallow, superficial and unreliable, but not everybody. In fact, chapter one of John ends with Jesus describing Nathaniel as an Israelite without any guile. Nicodemus proved himself and was the one man among the ruling leaders in Jerusalem to be true to Jesus and identify with Him after He was crucified (see John 19:39,40). Some seeds are sown without bearing fruit. Some bear a little, some bear more and some are very successful. The same seed, the same sower, but different ground. It all depends to whom you are preaching. Jesus had no success at all in one Samaritan town; in fact, the locals wouldn't allow Him even to spend the night there. Yet in Sychar it was different.

More than once in Africa, we have lost a great deal of money invested in a crusade that was canceled at the last minute by the government. We have seen riots like Paul saw in Ephesus (see Acts 19:23-34), but what does it matter? In the end, we shall overcome (see 1 John 4:4). Jesus promised it.

Paul often spoke of patience and perseverance; they are necessary virtues for any evangelist. But God alone gives them. Jesus exemplified them. And He says, "Follow me" (Matt. 4:19). Well, He has gone ahead. So somebody must follow Him. Why not you?

FAITH AND EVANGELISM

Following Jesus requires faith; in fact, to follow Him will be impossible without it. He who believes shall be saved (see Mark 16:16). Evangelism is a vital part of making that happen. The evangelist is there to cultivate faith in the hearts of people; but to do that well, he must first have real faith himself. Faith is contagious. You can't pass on what you haven't got. Unless you have measles you cannot infect anyone else. Faith is first caught, then taught. You got it from somebody else, and others will get it from you.

People talk about the evangelistic gift and debate what it really means. Simply put, the evangelistic gift is an infectious faith. To enthuse others we must be enthused ourselves. Voltaire said he didn't believe Christians were redeemed because they didn't *look* redeemed. Christian messengers are not just audiotapes—words only. They're more like videos—words with visuals. When Philip went to Samaria, the Bible tells us "there was great joy in that city" (Acts 8:8). The kind of faith on display in the life and preaching of Philip made people jubilant.

Faith in John's Gospel

The word "faith" is conspicuously missing from the Gospel of John. John seems to avoid it. Even in his three epistles the word occurs only once. This is surprising because the word "faith" (Greek: *pistis*) is found 244 times in the New Testament. Instead of the noun "faith," John chooses to use the verb "to believe" (Greek: *pisteuo*). Oddly, the other three Gospels don't use "believe" or "believing" much at all—only 11 times in Matthew, 15 times in Mark, 9 times in Luke—whereas it occurs exactly 100 times in the book of John.

"Faith" is an abstract concept. "Believe" describes an action. Faith can be static, but believing is dynamic. "Believing" is one word in John's Gospel that is important for any understanding of evangelism, but there is another word that must go along with it: "witnessing."

You might expect to find the word "gospel" or "evangelism" in John, but there is no mention of either word. Again, John chooses a different, more dynamic term: the verb "to witness" (Greek: *martureo*), sometimes translated as "testify." That particular Greek verb is used 33 times by John. Now these two words— "believing" and "witnessing"—represent something ongoing, active, not static. They are connected—while we are believing, we are also witnessing.

John never treats the gospel as just a doctrine, a definition of truth in words. He always refers to something happening. He knows the gospel is truth. In 2 John 9, he says, "Anyone who runs ahead and does not continue in the teaching of Christ does not have God; whoever continues in the teaching has both the Father and the Son." The Gospel of John is written to show that the gospel is a dynamic, ongoing happening. It is both truth and light. His readers see exactly where they are and exactly where they will go if they opt to believe in Jesus Christ.

John uses action words wherever possible. He speaks, for example, of the truth as something shining on and on, constantly lighting the world, not just a light that once shone. The *New International Version* offers the closest rendering of the original text of John 1:9: "The true light that gives light to every man was coming into the world." Again, John never speaks about "knowledge" of the gospel or "knowledge" of God; instead he talks about "knowing"—something you are in the process of *doing*. Christ is not someone you heard about or know about, but someone you are knowing, experiencing, in the here and now. He is with you.

To John, faith is alive. It is not a creed—something you accept—but something you do. As Smith Wigglesworth used to say, "Faith is an act."

A Living Faith

John's objective was to show that the Christian faith is a living thing, not a static religion. Christ is life; believing is life; knowing Him is life. The characteristics of life are reproduction and adaptation. The Bible itself is a fine example: It is the living Word. It reproduces itself in human experience. "The word of God grew and multiplied" (Acts 12:24, *NKJV*). It speaks and is a force in the world. Some think of the Word of God as nothing more than ancient documents that the Church has preserved—a kind of museum piece. It is nothing of the kind. *It lives*. Its activity is ongoing.

The Scriptures are with us today by virtue of being the "very words of God" (Rom. 3:2), not because the Church preserved them. The Bible preserved the Church. There are many societies for preserving things—the environment, ancient buildings, peace, the species, traditions and so on, but, thank God, there is no need of a Society for the Preservation of the Ancient Scriptures. Living things don't need to be preserved; only dead things are placed in preserving fluids.

In the New Testament, the word "preserve" is found only in the *King James* translation of 2 Timothy 4:18—"And the Lord shall deliver me from every evil work, and will preserve me unto his heavenly kingdom"—but the original Greek word *sozo* literally means "saved." We are saved, but we are not preserved. We have eternal life! We won't go to heaven as mummies or deep-frozen personalities. The palpitating life of eternity flows in our souls.

Our Role Is Clearly Defined

The gospel must be preached to make it the gospel. The word "gospel," as you probably know, comes from the Greek for good news, *euangelion*. If you keep news to yourself, it isn't news at all. News is information broadcast on an extensive scale. If you put news in a book on the shelf, it is then history. The gospel is not history, although it is historical truth. The gospel *happens*. It becomes news when it is preached. You may call it anything you like—theology, the Word, the Truth—but if it is not articulated, it is not good news and the word "gospel" doesn't fit. Faith is not a truth that can be enclosed within the covers of a theological dissertation, put on the shelf and called "the gospel." The truth of the gospel can, of course, be written down, but *the gospel is you and me telling the story of Christ*, whatever the chosen means of transmission.

We are stewards of the gospel, not its prison wardens. The steward has to disburse what he controls, not lock up treasures of truth protectively out of harm's way. Exposing the gospel to its enemies defends the faith best; it is fully capable of dealing with them. We are stewards assigned to dispense the good news with the liberality of God to all. The Church is not a strong room built to keep the truth intact, but "a philanthropic institution," a distribution center. Elisha gave a woman the never-failing jar of oil but God has given us an oil field, a gusher that will never dry out.

When faith and witness combine, it produces something like an explosion. Paul said the gospel is "the power of God" (Rom. 1:16). Proclaiming the gospel releases the power of God. Many people pray for power, but power is latent within the gospel itself. Preach the Word and power is unleashed.

There is said to be enough oxygen locked up in the rocks of Mars to restore its atmosphere. Well, there is enough "spiritual oxygen" stored in the gospel to restore this whole world! Preach it and the proclamation of Christ acts as a catalyst causing inter-action between the power of the Holy Spirit and those who hear the message. The Holy Spirit will act when Jesus is preached—for example, convicting people of sin. But it all begins with our believing, doing what we are supposed to do. Put your faith to work, preach the Word and God goes into action. That is the dynamic of the gospel.

What Is True Faith?

There are characters we could describe as "unbelieving believers." They are sound in doctrine but have no trust. They preach what they call the gospel, but it is lifeless, just a statement of their orthodoxy. When a man describes the beauty of a lovely girl, he can do so quite clinically. But if he is in love with her, then he makes her sound like a very alive person, worthy of drawing him into a relationship.

Preaching must in itself be a believing act, fully reliant on God. The truth of Christ is the seed we must sow. But without faith it is seed that has never been fertilized. The gospel won't germinate, spring up, blossom or produce fruit unless it is preached with faith. To have faith in the faith once delivered to the saints (see Jude 3) is very important, but it is not sufficient. Faith should be fruitful, life generating—"by believing you may have life in his name" (John 20:31). It is a vibrant, living process. You are believing, you are receiving, you are knowing, you are seeing, you are abiding in Him. The gospel is not truth on ice, but truth on fire.

Jesus did not say, "I am the way and the truth"; He said, "I am the way and the truth *and the life*" (John 14:6, emphasis mine). The outcome of believing is income from God: Ongoing faith enjoys incoming life.

The David and Goliath episode (see 1 Sam. 17) is a perfect example of the difference between active and passive faith. Israel had a faith. They declared that Jehovah was God. It was a tremendous truth for them. But they may just as well have said—and believed—that the moon was made of green cheese. Their statement of faith in Jehovah God may just as well not have been true, because it did nothing in their lives.

Here they were, a whole army with the king himself, a namby-pamby half-wit, as their field leader. They shouted the name of the Lord and made a fearful racket with their weapons. They believed they were the people of God, that He was on their side. But that's as far as it went. It didn't inspire one soldier to move out of the ranks to go one-on-one with Goliath. Of course, to do that required real faith, as nobody in Israel could hope to match Goliath physically, not even King Saul.

The shepherd boy David was an outsider. But he walked into the valley, was outraged by the giant's blasphemy and declared he would take Goliath's head off. And he did. "Faith without works is dead," exactly as the Bible tells us (Jas. 2:26, *NKJV*).

Evangelism calls for that kind of active believing. It is testifying, witnessing, seeing, knowing and doing. But we need some grounds for that kind of bold trust. Believing God has nothing to do with being naïve, credulous or ignorant. If you want faith, put it into action. The assurance of faith is like the assurance of swimming—you must act!

The God Who Never Changes

Faith in God rests on God's faithfulness. Lamentations 3:22,23 (*NKJV*) tells us, "His compassions fail not. They are new every morning; great is Your faithfulness." These are astonishing words. Jeremiah spoke them as he sat looking out over Jerusalem, which had been sacked and razed to the ground and left as a heap of smoldering rubble. He wept over that city. Yet He knew that God was faithful. Jeremiah's faith never faltered. Psalm 119:90 (*NKJV*) assures us: "Your faithfulness endures to all generations."

In what way is God faithful? To whom or what is He faithful? God is faithful to *Himself.* He is always what He says He is. He never lets Himself down by doing something different than what He really is. What He has revealed about His character is consistent with what He does; God never acts out of character. We can never say about anything He does, "That's not Him! He's not like that." Whatever He does *is* Him. He is what He says He is, and He does what He says He will. In fact, He *must* do certain things, if He is the God He says He is. The certainty of His promises rests on His faithfulness (see Num. 23:19).

More than once in John's Gospel, Jesus openly states what He must do. He had to do certain things because of who He was and is. Scripture says, "He cannot deny Himself" (2 Tim. 2:13, *NKJV*). He must act according to His nature. If His nature is love, then He must love. If He is righteous, then He must be just. God can only be what He is: namely, God. As a human being, I must breathe, eat and walk. God must care, act and save.

God revealed His true identity right from the very beginning. He said to Moses, "I AM WHO I AM" (Exod. 3:14). The experts have examined and discussed the range of this statement's possible meanings and implications. They have considered the words grammatically and theologically. But irrespective of these considerations, the meaning is plain enough. God is saying He is faithful—He is what He is and never changes. For instance, He linked His call of Moses to what He had been for previous generations, saying, "I have remembered my covenant, which I made with Abraham, Isaac and Jacob" (see Exod. 6:2-5). Four centuries had elapsed, but God had not conveniently forgotten what He had promised to those patriarchs. What He was then, He still was 400 years later. Pointing to the "I AM" known to Abraham, He could say to Moses without the faintest shadow of doubt, "I AM WHO I AM."

Whatever He does *once* shows what He is like forever. Every divine act is a sign and prophecy of things He will do in times to come. Whatever He does is an expression of His unchanging character. God Himself makes this clear: "I am the LORD, I do not change; therefore you are not consumed, O sons of Jacob" (Mal. 3:6, NKJV). Even in the face of the greatest possible provocation His attitude remains rock steady. He never changes. He is perfect and to depart from what He is would mean He is less than perfect.

Having faith in God means having faith that God is always what He has been. If He answers prayer once, we can rest assured that His natural response to prayer is to answer it. If He has ever cared for one person, it is because He always cares and will therefore care for all. If He heals one suffering individual, it is because

He is a healer; it is in His nature to heal people. If He forgives one repentant person, it is because He is the Forgiver. If He ever saved one human being, it is because He is God our Savior, whose desire it is for all men to be saved.

God Is Willing

God does what He does because he *wants* to do it. Even the first chapter of Genesis reveals a spontaneous God in action. At no time during the act of creation was He prompted to do what He did by any outside pressure or obligation. There wasn't a committee of angels standing nearby, suggesting that light might be a good thing, or saying, "What if there were a firmament dividing the waters?"

God didn't think to Himself, *Well, I suppose I had better make a world, a nice world. If I didn't, it wouldn't be right. People expect me to do better.* No such consideration ever affected Him. He didn't consult with His conscience or consider what future generations of people might think or what history would say. He simply wanted to create. It was His will, His wish, His instinct and His delight. What He wants to do is what He loves to do. There is nothing unpassionate about God. What He does, He does from the heart, with noble, open-handed generosity.

The gospel reflects God's spontaneous dynamism. When Adam fell, God did not let him stay there. He didn't hit him with a lecture on moral compromise and its devastating effects. God came to pick him up again, to rehabilitate and reassure him, to clothe him and promise him a future. That is God. We see that from the opening pages of the Bible. Indeed, that is what the Bible—the Old and the New Testaments—is about. From the very beginning we see God's unsolicited and total concern for mankind.

This theme is developed throughout the Old Testament. The principles we find in the Gospels are first seen in everything God does throughout the Old Testament. Israel becomes the canvas upon which He paints the picture of His character. From the first chapters of Genesis we see that:

1. The world was intended for good.
2. Creation is based on His goodness.
3. History will be shaped for good.
4. God and goodness will triumph over evil.

The Revelation of God in Jesus

The revelation of God comes in its fullest glory in Jesus Christ, which is why we preach Him (see John 1:18). It is He who interprets the God of the Old Testament. His astoundingly wonderful life reveals an astoundingly wonderful God. Jesus altered people's ideas of God by showing them who He really is.

God cannot be greater than Himself, and Jesus provided us with the highest possible conception of God. God is not interested in our philosophies, our reasonings about Him, however right or wrong they may be. We derive our knowledge of God's character entirely from His dealings with mankind. That is our evidence and all we need to know. God Himself loves us and has come to save us, and He wants us to know His glory.

We see Him most truly as He is for us when He hangs on the Cross. If you forget that, you know nothing about God. Anything beyond that is a matter of speculation and is of no lasting value. There may be other sides to God, since He is infinite. But we don't know what they are. Both the Old and the New Testaments make it clear that our knowledge of God is limited:

The secret things belong to the LORD our God, but the things revealed belong to us and to our children forever (Deut. 29:29).

For now we see in a mirror, dimly.... Now I know in part (1 Cor. 13:12, *NKJV*).

Nonetheless, He has made His intentions perfectly clear, and we interpret what He will do from what His accomplished deeds tell us about Himself.

The Revelation of God in Scripture

The Bible is our ultimate reference point if we are looking for the revelation of God. We can look at the Bible in many ways: as the book of salvation, the book of the Kingdom or the Word of life. But above and beyond all other considerations, the Bible is God's revelation of who He is, what He is and what we can expect of Him.

WE ONLY REALLY KNOW WHAT GOD IS LIKE FROM SCRIPTURE. THE BETTER WE UNDERSTAND THE BIBLE, THE BETTER WE UNDERSTAND GOD.

Faith is faith in the God of the Bible, not faith in some theory of our own of what God is or should be. Knowing that He is all-powerful, people will come to Him with a to-do list of 50 different tasks, many of which actually contradict one another! They will bless and curse their neighbor in the same breath. But God cannot contradict Himself because consistency is one facet of His character. He does not do a thing one minute and its opposite the next.

True faith is based on what God is like, and we only really know that from Scripture. The better we understand the Bible, the better we understand God. It is a lifetime employment. To understand Jesus, look at the Old Testament. What God is there, Jesus is in the New Testament and today. To understand the God of the Old Testament, look at Jesus in the New Testament. Jesus shows Jehovah's true nature.

We might get a different picture of God from the Old to the New Testament unless we appreciate the eternal faithfulness of God. He may change tactics. He comes to people as they are and shows Himself against the background with which they are familiar, but the light of His love still gets through even when it is filtered through a glass darkly.

The light that travels through clear air is the same light that radiates through a red sky, through dirty windows or through a prism. The light that came to Joshua was the same light that Moses saw in the burning bush and the same light the apostles saw on the Day of Pentecost. It is the same light that Saul saw on the Damascus road and which Abraham saw as a smoking lamp. God's love may come as anger or as judgment, but it is still love.

There is perfect unity between every revelation God makes about Himself in the Word. We may have to look for it, but it is there. That is why we constantly scan the Scriptures, to seek its inner core, its unity, which is the unfailing unity of God.

The Same Yesterday, Today and Forever

Jesus Christ is the same yesterday, today and forever (see Heb. 13:8) because God is changeless, irrespective of time and fashion. Faith is only possible if ours is a faithful God. If we can think of any reason why He should change, then our faith is a qualified faith.

Some people who call themselves dispensationalists believe that what God does depends on the era we are living in. Did God change halfway through the book of Acts, jumping from one epoch to another? Such an approach divides the Word of truth until one part has nothing to do with another part and the promises of God are itemized in separate watertight compartments. According to this view, God is not always the same from one time to the next, but is limited in what He can do by the current order of things.

If God is only the same under certain circumstances, then He is not changeless and circumstances change Him just as they change us. Human beings change with the passing of time, but God is not affected by time. Dividing the Word of God into times and seasons renders His faithfulness meaningless. Remember, "His truth endures to all generations."

If we must study precisely whether or not we have got Him in the right dispensational setting, our faith becomes controversial and unstable. Faith is not based on scriptural interpretations, but on the whole grand picture of what God has been from the beginning of time. Some only trust Him to do this or that if they have been persuaded that they are living in the right era. But it seems to me the Bible sends a very clear message: His faithfulness is not conditioned by the calendar.

God and Healing

In Genesis 20, we read the story of Abraham and Abimelech. This is the first healing story recorded in Scripture. The prayer of Abraham brought forgiveness and healing to the whole household of the Philistine chief, Abimelech. However, this was not Abraham's idea; it was the Lord's idea from the start. He told Abimelech to ask Abraham to pray for him to be healed.

That is the way God works, by prompting prayer. *When God wants to do a certain thing, He inspires prayer that He may do it. He only works that way.* He inspired Abraham to pray and inspired Abimelech to expect Abraham's prayer to be answered. It was all of God. And when He healed that household of this Philistine settler, a heathen man, God had committed Himself—He could never again be any different. God had revealed what He was, and He could not go back on it. God shows Himself by His deeds and His deeds do not stand in contrast to His nature.

God may not copy His own deeds exactly. He rarely repeats Himself, for He has an infinite store of new approaches and plans. He may not heal everybody, but He has shown Himself to be the Healer and that healing is what He wants to do. What His deeds demonstrate is the unchanging heart and character behind them. He has the same love, the same will He always has had, and His deeds cannot violate His character.

The Divine Imperative

As we have seen, what God is is what He *must* do. God cannot be what He is and *not* do it. If He is love, He *must* love somebody. If He is a Savior He *must* save. He *must* heal, because He has revealed Himself to be a healer.

In the Gospel of John, this comes out in the *imperatives* of Jesus. When Jesus said, "You must be born again" (John 3:7), He meant that He Himself must do it for us. We cannot rebirth ourselves. Only God can bring such a thing about. James 1:18 declares, "He chose to give us birth through the word of truth." Rebirth comes by the Word of truth, the gospel. If the world is to be saved, the people *must* hear the gospel. If they *must* hear the gospel, then somebody *must* preach it: "How can they hear without someone preaching to them?" (Rom. 10:14).

People need the gospel, and their need creates a need in the heart of God: He *needs* to send us with the gospel. He knows we must be born again, and He can't just sit down on His throne and do nothing about it. That would be completely contrary to all He has ever done. He knows our need and He is under compulsion to meet it.

Likewise, if we who are made in God's image know about the hungry in the world, we need to do something about it. Their need creates in us a need to help the needy. If you and I have plenty, then we cannot merely stand by and watch our neighbors die of starvation. The same is true of spiritual food. Our spiritual need lays a compulsion on the heart of God; our attitude toward others should be the same.

When Jesus said, "You must be born again," it meant that He also had to say almost immediately, "The Son of Man must be lifted up" (John 3:14). He used the same word, "must." Our need becomes His need to meet our need. Jesus lived under a constant sense of the imperative will of God. He must save because we need to be saved. He said, "I have other sheep," sheep that must be saved. "I must bring them also" (John 10:16).

This revelation of God becomes our basis for both faith and evangelism. The God of the Bible, our Lord Jesus Christ, the changeless One, will never let us down. We go at His bidding with our hand in His and we introduce Him to a weary world.

A Question of Relevance

Let me remind you that the initiative is not with us; it is with God. Behind everything is the moving Spirit of God. That being the case, *we are either relevant or irrelevant to what God is doing.*

God is our center; not this world. People say that we Christians are eccentric. An eccentric object wobbles around a point that is off-center. But that is what the Bible calls "the world." It is not believers, evangelists, witnesses or Christians who are eccentric, but the world. The world wobbles as it revolves around itself, but the believer is centered on God.

When people in the Church talk about making the gospel relevant, they usually mean that we need to show that the gospel has something in common with the world of industry, entertainment and commerce. *They have it backward.* The question is not whether the message can be related to this world, but whether the world is willing to relate to the message of the Cross. Too bad for the world if it is not, for it will be judged at the Cross. If the world is not relevant to the gospel, then the world is drifting; it has no anchor.

Another thing I hear people saying is that evangelists ask questions the world is not asking. Thank God for that! We are giving answers, ready for when the world decides to ask the right questions. Because it is asking all the wrong questions, any answers would be equally wrong.

Relevance is a matter of position and focus. *We are only relevant when we relate to what the Holy Spirit is doing.* We are often told our ministry has to be geared to the times. This is nonsense. We are geared to God. The machinery of heaven is turning, wheels within wheels. It is the machinery of heaven, not of industry, that must be our concern. To be geared to the world means turning our gospel into another form of materialism—just another way to rake in money and goods. What makes us relevant is not whether our message fits the situation—"Do not be conformed to this world," the Bible tells us (Rom. 12:2, *NKJV*)—but whether the situation corresponds to the truth of Christ. In fact, the world is of no importance if it does not relate to God.

We need to get our priorities right. We either get into the main-stream of revelation—the love of God for a wasted world—or we drift into a backwater filled with debris of theological controversy and church politics. Our priority must be the same as that of the Spirit. Why is the Holy Spirit here? The Holy Spirit is given to make us witnesses, and His own work is to highlight the work of Christ and actuate it in human lives (see John 16:9-11; Acts 1:8). If we want to move in the Spirit, we need to get into *that* kind of activity because that is what He is doing.

Some people who talk about moving *in* the Spirit seem to think and act as if they are the ones *moving* the Spirit. This is not biblical: "Who has directed the Spirit of the LORD, or as His counselor has taught Him?" (Isa. 40:13, *NKJV*). He is not moving secretly. He has not suddenly shot off in some new and unexpected direction only spotted by a few members of some spiritual elite. We still find God at work among people who are down: the sinful, the hopeless and the derelicts. Follow Jesus—that is a better expression than moving in the Spirit. Follow Him and you will go where He goes, doing good and healing all who are oppressed by the devil (see Acts 10:38).

PREACHING A
MIRACLE CHRIST

Unless we grasp the revelation of Jesus as the divine Son of God, we will never see His power released for ministry. Somebody wrote a book about Jesus entitled *The Man Nobody Knows*. I remember, of course, that Jesus Himself said, "No one knows the Son except the Father, and no one knows the Father except the Son and those to whom the Son chooses to reveal him" (Matt. 11:27). Jesus is referring to the mystery of God in the flesh, which is beyond our human comprehension. But we can know Him as Savior and Lord, even if we cannot grasp His infinite greatness.

There are different degrees of knowing people, which does not necessarily mean that we can fathom their nature. People may be commonly heard to say, "I just don't understand my wife!" We can know God Himself, but only to the extent that Jesus reveals Him. Scripture makes knowing Him a vital part of salvation: If we are saved, we know God.

In the words of Paul, made famous in the old hymn, I can say, "I know whom I have believed" (2 Tim. 1:12, *KJV*). I know what He is and who He is. To know Him is "life eternal," an ever-unfolding wonder. We can "grow in the grace and knowledge of our Lord and Savior Jesus Christ" (2 Pet. 3:18). We get to know God better as time goes by, but His basic character remains unchanged. It is true that now we see "through a glass, darkly, and not face to face" (see 1 Cor. 13:12, *NKJV*); but meanwhile what He means to me is everything.

Which Christ Are We Preaching?

When you preach Christ, the question is, *which* Christ? Above all, it should be a Christ you can know. I call Him "my Christ," "my Lord," "my God." Throughout the New Testament men and women had a relationship with Jesus. Typical of them was Mary Magdalene. She held His feet and cried, "Rabboni," or my Lord (John 20:16). In the same chapter, the apostle Thomas cried out, "My Lord and my God" (v. 28).

Paul spoke of Jesus with the same intimate affection as Mary. He said, "The life which I now live . . . I live by faith in the Son of God, who loved me and gave Himself for me" (Gal. 2:20, *NKJV*). Many of us can easily relate to these people in respect to our personal feelings about Jesus. Many say things like "He is my Savior" or "He is mine, this wonderful Savior." The Jesus I know is so wonderful I can't help talking about Him. This Jesus is the one who died on the cross for me, which is why I preach "Christ and Him crucified" (1 Cor. 2:2).

However, there are new "Christs" now on offer that the world has never known before. The Jesus some people talk about doesn't seem to be One I recognize, whose face "was marred more than any man" (Isa. 52:14, *NKJV*). In fact, I can't imagine

Christ belonging to anybody at all, the way some describe Him. He is often pictured as a dead Christ, perhaps lying across the lap of His living mother; as a babe helpless in her arms; or hanging dead on the cross. That is not a Christ with whom one can have any kind of personal relationship. There are many representations of Jesus like that—ones I can't use the relative pronoun "my" about.

New theologies talk about the political Christ, the revolutionary Christ, the liberal Christ, the humanist Christ, the Christ of religion (sitting unperturbed like Buddha forever), the historical Christ, a great untouchable Deity and so on.

The Jesus I know is very different.

He is a warm, caring Jesus whom I can love. I don't just admire Him, like some distant mountain or a star; that would not be someone I could call "my Jesus."

The Search for Historical Jesus

Many recent studies of Jesus have one thing in common: They strip Him of all that is supernatural—no virgin birth, no miracles, no physical resurrection, no ascension. Christ was stripped once before (and crucified) and now people are trying to take from Him every element that makes His death the victory it was. The Jesus whom people have adored and died for was the wonder-working Jesus who healed them and made them new creatures. He was a miracle Himself, born the Son of a virgin. He was crucified but became the conqueror of death. We must preach *that* Jesus. I don't care what scholars may say. I know Him. I know what He is to me and I know what He can do.

No ordinary mortal could save us from the flames of hell. That is the work of God incarnate. Christ penetrated the central court of the cosmos and met the demands of infinite justice. He came from the presence of the Judge of all, presenting the documents of my pardon and forgiveness, signed and sealed. The One who could move in that dimension could be nothing less than a miracle Christ.

People want and need more than a political revolutionary with a social gospel or a religious leader with a new system. More than an ethical Christ. More than a sublime heavenly Spirit. People want the divine Christ who could bear our sins in His own body on the tree (see 1 Pet. 2:24).

We don't get our Christ from historians alone. Whether Flavius Josephus mentions Him or not does not matter at all. He is not a Jesus the historians tell us about—a mere Jesus of history. For a century or so scholars have tried to portray Jesus as a great historical figure, but without the supernatural. I am sure you will also know that in his famous book *The Quest of the Historical Jesus* (1910), Dr. Albert Schweitzer demolished the idea that Jesus was just an ethical teacher. And Dr. Schweitzer was no evangelical, but searched for evidence for the erroneous teaching in great piles of books. Dozens of scholars had tried to piece together the Jesus of history as just a teacher without miracles. But, as Dr. Schweitzer observed, there was no agreement among them.

It is impossible to separate Jesus from His divinity and miraculous powers. Almost all we know of Him is presented to us in a supernatural framework. Take away the miracle element and the story falls apart. Healings are not incidentals, little bits of magic added in here and there. They are the very substance of the Gospels. John, for example, gives us a book full of signs and says, "These [signs] are written that you may believe that Jesus is the Christ, the Son of God" (John 20:31, *NKJV*). Picture Jesus without the miraculous and what do we end up with? "The Man Nobody Knows."

Jesus is far more than a figure of history. He came from outside the fabric of time and space, invaded history and changed it. He is the key, the focal point of all history. History either relates to Him or it doesn't make sense. He explains it all. Nothing adds up without Him. Christ is the linchpin of creation.

I read in newspapers about the Jesus Seminars, 43 unbelieving scholars who appointed themselves experts, deciding what Jesus did and didn't do, what He said and didn't say, which parts of the Gospels we can throw out and which ones we can safely keep. They are still playing the same game, with the same circular reasoning, as scholars in the age of Dr. Schweitzer. They want to remove from the Gospels everything that makes Jesus different and then say He is no different from anyone else! What peculiar logic! They write off any miraculous evidence as unhistorical so as to draw a picture of the historical Jesus.

I only pay them the compliment of mentioning them at all because they have been given enormous publicity. The godless press is delighted with their "findings," of course. The members of the Jesus Seminars find little of Him that they think true. At best they consider Him a harmless, wandering preacher who, for some reason or other, after His death inspired many impossible legends. In fact, these self-appointed authorities are sure of nothing. One of them has stated he believes there is only one single statement that we can feel reasonably sure may be attributed to Christ.

You probably know all about that controversy. I mention it for one reason only: We either must believe in a Christ of the supernatural, a signs-and-wonders Jesus who was the Son of God, or we have no reason for giving Him a second thought. However wonderful His ethics, without the miraculous there is no divine dynamic. The Sermon on the Mount becomes a more difficult mountain to climb than Everest.

We should clearly understand that the four Gospels are the Word of God and are written that way. They are not fond emotional reminiscences. We don't get our Jesus from history, and no amount of historical research can take Him away. There are no books in the world like the Gospels. These are not just accounts giving the kinds of details as might be given about Bismarck. They are revelations of the Holy Spirit that tell us about Jesus, and we need the Holy Spirit to open our eyes to interpret them. In other words, we need precisely the same revelation as Peter, who knew who Jesus was not by flesh and blood but by the Father in heaven (see Matt. 16:17).

The beginnings and endings of the Gospels are remarkable. No other books start and finish like these. The Gospel of Matthew begins with Christ as the Son of David and ends with His ascension to all power. Mark begins with Jesus as the Son of God and ends with the resurrected Jesus going everywhere with His disciples. Luke begins with Jesus as the son of Mary and Joseph and ends with Jesus in glory. John begins with Him as the Word in the beginning with God and ends with Jesus having a meal on a beach with His disciples. These beginnings and endings alone show us we have a Christ to preach who transcends all human life. There is no Christian faith left if this miracle element is discarded. Our gospel is either supernatural or we must abandon it. But we don't abandon it, because it produces supernatural results.

Jesus Today

The Christ of the Gospels is the Christ we need. If we preach Christ, we must preach the true Christ and not a Christ who is different from the record. If we don't preach a Jesus who heals, for instance, we are not preaching the same Christ of the

Gospels. His miracles were His "I.D." This is who He is, and He still carries that I.D. His ascension to heaven in no way changed His character. His miracles still attest to His identity. How can it be known that our Jesus is the biblical Jesus if He performs no more mighty works?

The first verse of the Acts of the Apostles says, "In my former book, Theophilus, I wrote about all that Jesus began to do and to teach." The use of the word "began" in respect to Jesus' activities quite clearly indicates that He continues to work. In this sense, the Acts of the Apostles is really a portrait of Christ still at work. If we preach Him still as being the Savior, we must still preach Him, too, as being the Healer. As the book of Acts shows, the Jesus of the Gospels exercised power in the physical world, not just in the spiritual realm.

The book of Revelation comes from "Him who is, and who was, and who is to come" (1:4). We can know Him as He always was, because He continues to do the same as He always did. We may be able to recognize a geographical landmark though it does nothing. But in order to recognize people, we need to see them alive and in action. That is how we recognize Jesus—by what He does. If He no longer does what He once did, how can we be sure it is Him?

Hebrews 13:8 declares that He is the same yesterday, today and forever. Many people claim to believe that verse, but then they turn around and say that He doesn't do what He used to do! They quote the text, but then they qualify it. We have no right to qualify the Word of God. We must remember when we talk about miracles and supernatural healings that these were not incidentals in His life. They constituted a basic ministry of Jesus Christ, as Peter observed: "He went around doing good and healing all who were under the power of the devil" (Acts 10:38). If I know Jesus at all, I can never believe that He would renege on

His mercies to mankind. So many people trust Him; He would never let them down. The need is as great as ever it was, and the Jesus I know would never ignore it.

The Anointed One

On His return to His hometown of Nazareth, Jesus read from Isaiah 61:1, "The Spirit of the Lord is on me, because he has anointed me to preach good news to the poor. He has sent me to proclaim freedom for the prisoners and recovery of sight for the blind, to release the oppressed, to proclaim the year of the Lord's favor" (Luke 4:18,19). Having read these words, He then told those gathered to hear him speak, "Today this scripture is fulfilled in your hearing" (v. 21). On this important occasion Jesus declared Himself to be the Anointed One, the Christ.

The anointing in question is specially related to His ministry of healing and deliverance. Peter told the household of Cornelius, "God anointed Jesus of Nazareth with the Holy Spirit and power, and . . . he went around doing good and healing all who were under the power of the devil, because God was with him" (Acts 10:38).

Today, He is still Christ, still the Anointed One, with the same purpose: to deliver and heal the oppressed. Whenever we call Him Christ, we use a code word for His healing ministry. If anyone reading this believes He does not heal today, then why call Him Christ? What sort of Christ is the One who doesn't heal?

. Salvation, forgiveness and physical healing are closely linked in Scripture. Jesus forgave sin and removed the judgment upon sin. Healing is a sign of forgiveness. The name of Jesus means salvation from sin (see Matt. 1:21), and the name of Christ is inextricably linked to physical deliverance. No Scripture tells me that Jesus Christ is *not* the same yesterday, today and forever—just the opposite! His miracles are not only illustrations of spiritual salvation, they are promises that He will do the same things today. It is false to divide body and soul and make salvation apply to the soul but not the body. Salvation is for the whole person.

Church History and the Miraculous

As a brief aside, I would like to refer to Dr. Benjamin Warfield of Princeton Theological Seminary. As you may know, he was an astute evangelical theologian, but he is presently used as an important proponent of the "no-miracles gospel."

Warfield insisted that miracles ended with the death of the apostles, one of his main arguments being that Church history has no record of the miraculous after about A.D. 100. This puzzles me. The nineteenth and twentieth centuries are as much a part of Church history as the second or third century. Indeed, the Church has seen its greatest expansion ever during the last hundred years. This has proven to be a very significant part of Church history. The fact is that that expansion has come about largely through the preaching of the full, miraculous gospel. *If there was a lack of signs and wonders before, that is no reason to deny them now. Why should unbelieving centuries impose their dead hand upon the present world revival?*

Furthermore, it is not accurate to say that the early centuries were devoid of the miraculous. It is not my particular field, but many who read the early fathers tell us the post-apostolic centuries were *not* devoid of miraculous healings. Jesus never lost His compassion for the sick. Even if there had been a cessation of the miraculous, it would prove nothing when healings are common worldwide today. Jesus is certainly still busy.

Let me add my humble experience and testify to what is happening during our own crusades. We are seeing the Acts of the Apostles repeated today—more than repeated. Scenes that were impossible 2,000 years ago are common experiences today because of modern means of communication that make far greater multitudes accessible. Not only the blind, the deaf, the diseased, the lame and the demon-possessed are being set free, just as in apostolic times, but converts counted by thousands on the Day of Pentecost are now counted by the tens of thousands, even hundreds of thousands. Every day some 150,000 are added to the Church worldwide, not 3,000 or 5,000.

Perhaps I could venture just one further comment on Dr. Warfield. Here is a Bible teacher and theologian of great distinction. He hammered it home that the Bible is the only source of doctrine, yet he turned to the human records of Church history to decide biblical truth. This to me, to say the least, seems very odd. The Bible has preeminence as the inspired Word of God and is to be used to interpret history, and not history to interpret the Bible.

Back to the Great Commission

William Carey, the father of modern missions, challenged the eighteenth-century Baptists and their theology. They said God would save whom He wanted to save and didn't need us to busy ourselves with it. Carey's point was that if we want the promises which go with the Great Commission, we must carry out the Great Commission. He was right. But what does the Great Commission have to do with signs and wonders? Let me show you.

Matthew 28:18-20 is the classic expression of the Great Commission. It commands us, "Go and make disciples of all nations." But it begins like this: "Jesus came to them and said,

'All authority ["power" in the *KJV*] in heaven and on earth has been given to me. *Therefore* go and make disciples'" (emphasis mine). He only sent His disciples when there was power—heavenly authority—*available*. This was not power reserved for operation in the realm of the purely spiritual, but power *on earth*; in other words, power that brings physical results.

Mark 16:15,17,18 makes it absolutely clear that the disciples were to expect miracles to accompany their task.

> He said to them, "Go into all the world and preach the good news to all creation. And these signs will accompany those who believe: In my name they will drive out demons; they will speak in new tongues; they will pick up snakes with their hands; and when they drink deadly poison, it will not hurt them at all."

Luke 24:47,49 reveals that Jesus told His disciples to wait for this miracle power before setting out on their mission: "Repentance and forgiveness of sins will be preached in [my] name to all nations. I am going to send you what my Father has promised; but stay in the city until you have been clothed with power from on high."

The Gospel of John clearly tells us that Jesus actually expected us to do the kinds of miracles that He did while He was on earth—and more!

> I tell you the truth, anyone who has faith in me will do what I have been doing. He will do even greater things than these, because I am going to the Father (John 14:12).

> As you sent me into the world, I have sent them into the world (John 17:18).

"As the Father has sent me, I am sending you." And with that he breathed on them and said, "Receive the Holy Spirit" (John 20:21,22).

Power and witnessing are definitely linked in Acts 1:8, in which Jesus says, "You will receive power when the Holy Spirit comes on you; and you will be my witnesses . . . to the ends of the earth."

In the letters of the apostles we find a similar expectation of power linked with the proclamation of the gospel. Scores of texts could be quoted, such as Paul's references to preaching with the demonstration of the Spirit (see 1 Cor. 2:4). If we fulfill the Great Commission, we have every right to expect the promises to be fulfilled, with signs following. *If we do what God says, God will do what He says.*

The Kingdom

The supernatural is the great evidence of the kingdom of God. *Where the Kingdom is, miracle power is seen.* This is important. Perhaps I ought to look briefly at the question of the kingdom of God first.

The great difference between the times before Christ and the times after Christ is the *abiding presence* of the Holy Spirit. On occasions, the Spirit came upon individuals as recorded in the Old Testament. Men like Moses, Elijah, Elisha, Samson and Gideon experienced the power of the Holy Spirit from time to time. The prophets spoke as they were moved, but nobody had known the baptism in the Holy Spirit until Jesus came, and from Him flowed the most extraordinary stream of miracles the world had ever witnessed. Before His death and resurrection, Jesus said that He would send His Spirit to be with the disciples at all times (see John 14:16,17). After the Day of Pentecost the Holy Spirit was resident in the Church.

The results were mighty works of power that had never been known before. The blind, deaf and crippled were restored—events never once recorded in the Old Testament. One other thing: demons were not cast out until Jesus cast out spirits with His word. That particularly became an evidence of a great change in the divine economy. Jesus said, "If I drive out demons by the finger of God, then the kingdom of God has come to you" (Luke 11:20). When demons were expelled at Christ's word, it was more than a sign of God's finger at work; it showed that the Kingdom was present.

> THE MIRACULOUS IS AN ESSENTIAL
> FEATURE OF THE KINGDOM OF GOD.
> IF THE KINGDOM IS AMONG US,
> THERE WILL BE WONDERS.

In other words, the miraculous is an essential, ongoing feature of the kingdom of God. If the Kingdom is among us, there will be wonders. If there are wonders, the Kingdom is among us. Christ's kingdom got a foothold on earth when Jesus came and Kingdom powers began working. The validating "stamp" of the Kingdom are signs and wonders. We definitely should not deny them and there is certainly no need to drum them up. I have long found them to follow the preaching of the Word.

Having said that, let me add a caveat. All sorts of people today are clamoring for the supernatural. Many are running from church to convention to conference hoping to see signs and sensations. Is that all Christianity is, mere supernaturalism?

There is far more in the gospel than curing the sick. The great works of God include salvation, building up the Church, and the believer manifesting the fruits of the Spirit in his or her life and being changed from day to day into the likeness of Jesus. The fellowship of the saints is another thing, but if we only wander around looking for signs and wonders, fellowship means nothing. Healing the sick means also sharing one another's burdens, and to do that we need to *know* people and their burdens.

Now we come to four Kingdom principles of great significance for all Christian work:

1. *Jesus can only be what you preach Him to be.*
The first of these four principles contains the germ of the other three, and I hope it will be one thing you take away from this book. Jesus waits for us to say what He is. Preach Him as the Savior and He saves. If you don't, He can't! Preach Him as a healer and He heals. If you don't, He doesn't! Preach Him as a forgiver, or as the giver of peace, then He can be these things to those who hear. Preach the gospel, and the gospel happens.

But give a little moral essay, leaning chattily on one elbow on the reading desk, and the only miracle taking place will be a cure for insomnia, because that kind of "pep talk" is enough to make anyone go to sleep!

If you preach a miraculous Jesus, He will *be* a miraculous Jesus. The Holy Spirit can only bless the truths which you allow Him to bless. He can't bless the truth of divine healing to anybody if you only talk about divine transcendence. If when sharing your faith your regular subject is hell, this rather limits the Holy Spirit. When you feel no anointing, perhaps the Holy Spirit is waiting for you to say something which He *can* anoint: His truth, clearly communicated.

2. *God's sovereign will is worked out through us.*

Mark's Gospel tells us that after he had ascended to heaven, Jesus "worked with" his disciples (Mark 16:20). We often talk about God's sovereign will, but He works His sovereign will through us, usually requiring us to do something first. Sovereignty does not mean secret; the word is grossly misunderstood and misused, and in any case it is not in the Bible. God is indeed our sovereign Lord and God, but he is not unpredictable. If we don't know God's will, then we certainly ought to. His Word is His will. Psalm 103 declares, "He made known His ways to Moses, His acts to the children of Israel" (Ps. 103:7, *NKJV*). If God were wholly unpredictable, we could not possibly have any faith in Him. We can depend on His holy, impeccably divine character.

In His sovereignty, God has planned to let us have a say in matters. "Shall I hide from Abraham what I am doing?" (Gen. 18:17, *NKJV*). He does more than that. Jesus said, "Ask whatever you will, and it shall be done for you" (John 15:7, *RSV*); the only proviso is that *we remain in Him.* God not only told Abraham what He wanted to do, but listened to Abraham's objections and even agreed to his wishes, as in the story of Sodom and Gomorrah (see Gen. 18:16-33). He also revealed His secrets to His servants, the prophets: "Surely the Lord GOD does nothing, unless He reveals His secret to His servants the prophets" (Amos 3:7, *NKJV*).

Generally speaking, the times when God burst upon the scene with little warning to anyone except His prophets is over. He may still do this now, but that is not His normal and regular way. The revelation of God in Jesus has ended that period of unpredictability. It is His sovereign will to go along with our will, though the Word of God must always condition our will. Of, course, He reserves the right to act independently and sometimes He may do so, but generally we beget His action by our action.

Perhaps there is no greater example of this principle than the life of William Carey, the famous missionary to India. He was a young English minister, burning with the thought of Christ's Great Commission. Yet there was nobody leaving England to go onto foreign fields. On one occasion he suggested to a group of Baptist ministers that they discuss this subject: "Whether the command given to the apostles to teach all nations was not binding on all generations." The chairman of the group, Elder Ryland, replied to his proposal in words that have been quoted a million times since as an example of wrongheaded, die-hard traditionalism: "Young man, sit down! You are an enthusiast. When God pleases to convert the heathen, he'll do it without consulting you or me."

Elder Ryland's ideas were typical of the times. God was thought to do what He wanted without consulting anybody or being prompted. This was the theory, too, behind revival, that it was a sovereign act of God, coming how, when and where the grace of God happened to choose with no apparent motivation or reason. The belief was that God came upon an area, saved who He wanted to save and then moved on until the next revival. Carey responded by publishing a tract which showed that we were not relieved of responsibility in the matters of evangelism and revival. William Carey went to India in 1793.

I can understand the frustration felt by William Carey. I too was a missionary, carrying out missionary duties in the traditional way. But I wanted to reach more people, much more quickly before they died. We were using nail scissors to reap the harvest one stem at a time, but I felt we needed combine harvesters. I was told that traditional missions was the proper way to reach the unsaved, that it had been well tried and was the most effective method. My soul found no rest, however, until I took the step which began the Christ for All Nations ministry.

Then I saw more converts in one night than a whole African mission station saw in a hundred years.

3. God works according to the scale we employ. Our measure of work is His.

Consider the widow who had a jar of oil. Elisha told her to get as many vessels as she could. She begged and borrowed vessels and filled them all until there were no more. God can fill as many vessels as we bring to Him. He can save as many souls and heal as many bodies as we give Him the chance to save and heal. He can have a parish outlook or a world outlook.

4. God always takes the initiative, but He expects us to follow.

He is the Captain of our faith (see Heb. 2:10, *NKJV*). Let me hark back to John's Gospel again. We read that Jesus healed some people without being specifically asked. Whatever miracles He performed came from God's own spontaneous desire: "The Son can do nothing by himself; he can do only what he sees his Father doing, because whatever the Father does the Son also does. For the Father loves the Son and shows him all he does" (John 5:19,20).

He made water into wine at no one's suggestion (see 2:1-10). He healed the nobleman's servant as He wanted, not as the nobleman said (see 4:46-53). He healed the sick man at the pool of Bethesda without the man asking (see 5:1-9). He restored a blind man by smearing clay in his eyes without so much as a "by your leave" (see 9:1-7). He turned down the request of Martha and Mary to visit their sick brother and came according to His Father's timetable, four days after Lazarus had died. It was Jesus' idea to raise Lazarus from the dead, nobody else's (see 11:1-44). The book of John is a grand illustration of God's absolute independence from the will of man.

At the start of any new thing God does, the thought is always His, not human promotion. That is why Jesus stressed that if we abide in Him and His words abide in us, He will do whatever we ask of Him (see John 15:7). However, God only takes the initiative. He will not proceed further until we first move in faith. Acting spontaneously and unprompted, He shows what He is and what He will do. He then expects us to step up and act upon that demonstration. That is what acting in faith means. It means we trust God to be what He has shown Himself to be. When Gideon asked, "Where are all His mighty miracles?" he assumed God would be again what He once showed Himself to be (see Judg. 6:13).

God never gets in on our act unless we have gotten in on *His* act. He always first shows us what He is and what He will do. Then it is up to us. He expects us to take His cue and act on it.

Paul said that he declared "the whole counsel of God" (Acts 20:27, *NKJV*). The word used for "counsel" can also be translated "will" or "desire." To declare His whole counsel is to declare His will. We couldn't declare His will if it were eternally closed to us and God were to do just what He wants whenever He wants without any rhyme or reason. God doesn't act on a whim. That is why the cry of our hearts should be that we should know the "good and acceptable and perfect will of God" (Rom. 12:2, *NKJV*).

If you will declare His whole Word, His whole counsel, without expunging selected texts as outside our current dispensation, then you have a supernatural God on your hands. Because He is Spirit and we are physical in a material world, anything we know of Him could only come supernaturally. We cannot preach the true Christ without the supernatural.

CHAPTER

6

THE ANOINTING FOR THE MISSION

Believing in a miraculous Christ releases faith into our lives to be His witnesses. That is what we are called to do as His *disciples*. When Christ commissioned His followers, He meant them not only to do something but to *be* something. His witnesses are samples of what He does. Marshall McLuhan made popular the notion that the medium is the message. Indeed, believers are the message of the gospel! We do not merely possess an intellectual knowledge of biblical truth; Christ imparts in us a burning faith that will testify of Him to the world.

Christians are not self-made. "We are His workmanship, created in Christ Jesus for good works" (Eph. 2:10, *NKJV*). The word "workmanship" literally means "product." We are His products. The new men, the new women we have become were created "in true righteousness and holiness" (Eph. 4:24). The supreme

Sculptor has fashioned us for all to see. We are His exhibits—testimony to His talents.

We are called to a ministry of *declaration*. The Holy Spirit within us is the Spirit of witness, of testimony, and witness is His specific work (see John 15:26). The gift of the Spirit is not given for us to play power games. His power shapes and forms us to be creatures of His purposes, not our purposes, as Revelation 4:11 (*KJV*) makes clear: "Thou hast created all things, and for thy pleasure they are and were created."

We are called to an eternal sense of *destiny*. What God has made us places upon us an obligation to fulfill the purpose for which we were formed. Our attitude should be that of Paul:

> But when God, who set me apart from birth and called me by his grace, was pleased to reveal his Son in me so that I might preach him among the Gentiles, I did not consult any man (Gal. 1:15,16).

Notice Paul's expression that it pleased God to "reveal His Son in me." As soon as He was born of God, He did what He was born to do. A bird is born to fly, a fish to swim, a human being to walk and talk, and a Christian is born again to witness. Witnesses should witness; it is our nature. Soldiers are not fitted with uniforms and equipped with weapons simply to go on parade; their true place is on the battlefield.

Although God plants the instinct of witness within us, He does not coerce us; we are not programmed robots and He is not a dictator. It is simply a test of our loving submission to Him. We can witness or not, as we choose. It is left to us, or rather left to our sense of what God wants and our awareness of the desperate plight of unregenerate people. Ephesians 4:23—5:2 (*NKJV*) encourages us: "Be renewed! . . . Put on the new man. . . . Walk in love." *We should serve because we are equipped to serve.*

It has been said, and rightly so, that the Great Commission is not the Great Suggestion. It is a draft, a call-up. It is a priority, the basic requirement of every church. We might ask this question: Has a church any right to exist if it does not carry out the purpose for which it exists? God's word to the indifferent Laodiceans is clear: "Because you are . . . neither cold nor hot, I will vomit you out of My mouth" (Rev. 3:16, *NKJV*). Jesus didn't say, "If you don't mind, and if you have some spare time, you might think about doing something for Me." *Doing God's will has nothing to do with doing Him a favor.* To be called to His service, to wear the livery of Christ, is the proudest honor a person can know.

There is an imperative in the heart of Jesus which transfers itself to those who belong to Him. We are here on earth in His place. He said, "You did not choose me, but I chose you and appointed you to go and bear fruit—fruit that will last" (John 15:16). Our business is not to be busy but to witness. Wherever we are, *what* we are doesn't change. An American is an American, whatever he does or wherever he goes. He has a living to earn, a family to support, perhaps a business to run, and he can be identified all over the world because he speaks English with an American accent. Christians are Christ's witnesses in exactly the same way. We are what we are. At all times, our lifestyle and accent of faith reveal to whom we belong. We belong to Christ.

The Anointing Equips

We are anointed, equipped for the task to which Christ has called us. This anointing is all-important. In 1 John 2:20,27 (*NKJV*) we read, "You have an anointing from the Holy One. . . . The anointing which you have received from Him abides in you."

The word "anointing" is the Greek *chrisma*, from which we get the word "Christ," the Anointed One. This "chrism," the endowment of the Holy Spirit, is the secret of a true evangelist.

Even Jesus Himself needed to receive the anointing to go about doing good and healing people. Now why would Jesus, the only begotten Son of God, need an anointing? He was flesh and blood, that is why. So are we. It is the anointing which takes our voice and our gestures and adds to them a special quality. No actor can imitate it. Watch an unconverted actor preaching in a television drama and it is so obviously artificial, like hearing a ventriloquist's doll. There's no soul in it. But true anointing from God breaks the yoke of sin.

First Thessalonians 5:19 (*NKJV*) tells us, "Do not quench the Spirit." Some have suggested that it is all too easy to quench the Spirit. Personally, I don't believe it. The Holy Spirit is not as touchy as that. The Holy Spirit is very persistent, powerful and working within us. He is the faithful One, the abiding One. How then can we quench the Spirit? The Spirit is given us to make us witnesses; if we are not interested in His objectives, *then* we quench the Spirit. What we have to do is to maintain the glow! The same word "quench" (Greek, *sbennumi*) was used by the five foolish virgins who said their lamps had gone out. We quench the Spirit when we cease shining for Christ.

Do We Need Replenishing?

There's an important question which has inspired controversy within Pentecostal circles: *Do we need to seek God from time to time to replenish the power of the Spirit?* Some of our songs imply as much: "Spirit of the living God, fall afresh on me. Melt me, mold me, fill me, use me." When God has broken and melted us, molded and filled us, how often must the process be repeated?

Do we need frequently to be broken, and must we be broken again every time we want to be filled?

This topic has been discussed at length among theologians. Those capable of doing so have quoted the tenses of Greek verbs to prove their points. I do not profess to aspire to that level of scholasticism. My approach comes from quite a different angle— simpler, but I trust not elementary.

If I knew I was empty of the Spirit and power, I would certainly seek God for refilling. But how would I know? I suppose there are two ways: first, that I would be ineffective in my work and second, that I would *feel* empty.

The first evidence of being powerless is not entirely reliable, because there are Spirit-filled people who are not having great success sowing the gospel seed on concrete. Lack of success and other stresses may cause them to become discouraged. They blame themselves and feel they must labor hard with God to be replenished. Of course, they are still unsure of whether they are "filled," because they have no way of knowing they're replenished unless they experience sudden and astounding breakthroughs. However, success—even hundreds or thousands of conversions— will not tell you whether you are Spirit-filled. So, if you are using successful evangelistic efforts as a measuring stick and if there is no change in your visible success rate after you have prayed and fasted, been on a retreat and had hands laid upon you, you will be left with nothing more than a vague hope that you have been filled again. This is a dangerous and discouraging way to live.

Before the twentieth-century Pentecostal revival began, the expectation of results as a sign of being Spirit-filled was pretty much how things were. With the coming of the charismatics and the Pentecostal revival, tongues were seen as the sign. If people could speak in tongues, then they knew they had received the Spirit. Without a sign people are never sure.[1]

Before the Pentecostal revival, the Church had many songs of aspiration and few of realization. People were always praying for power, singing, "Showers of blessing we need," "Let some drops now fall on me," "We want another Pentecost," "Revive Thy work, O Lord" or "Fill my cup, Lord."

The songs changed with those early twentieth-century Pentecostals. They sang, "Falling! Falling! Showers of latter rain!" or "'Tis Pentecost in my soul." The song I like is "He abides, He abides, the Comforter abides with me!"

What About Feelings?

Now, we may think we need another filling, but how do we know? By our feelings, obviously. We don't *feel* filled. But does the Spirit-filled Christian necessarily feel filled? Are feelings anything to go by at all?

Feelings are physical or psychological. If you are tired, have influenza, have suffered bereavement, were in a car accident or were beaten up like Paul often was, it is very questionable whether you would *feel* full of the Holy Spirit. Feelings are simply no criteria whatsoever. I can't say I felt I was brimming over with Holy Spirit power when the army had to protect us from mob violence in Nigeria in 1991.

Some people have superanxieties about whether God is with them. They lay down their own ground rules, which they believe are needed, then spend their days wondering if they have broken them. Have they missed hearing God's voice? Have they sinned or disobeyed? Have they stepped off the path of His will? And just when did that happen? They are constantly looking over their shoulders, analyzing the past to see if, by any chance, they have offended the Holy Spirit. In fact, what this means is that they are *never* sure about their relationship with God. These are the same people who are always wondering if they are humble enough, loving enough, good enough or if they are praying enough. They pray in hope, but not in faith.

Many such people are victims of their own legalistic outlook. Perfectionism is based on the mistaken idea that this side of heaven we can fulfill the requirements of the law. Perfectionism is not power but pride. Some strive for the unreachable; they want the self-satisfaction of their own holiness. Grace occupies a very small place in their expectations. For some people, grace has no place at all, except to acknowledge that they are saved by grace. They live under their own self-imposed law and see the fullness of the Spirit as a testimony to the achievements of their own holiness. There are those who pray for revival but know 50 reasons why it "tarries"—all of them having to do with the quality of Christian character of those involved. When revival still tarries, they can always find yet more reasons why it does. It is easy: Nobody is that perfect.

NOTHING IN SCRIPTURE INDICATES THAT GOD'S SPIRIT CAN BE FRIGHTENED OFF LIKE A NERVOUS DOVE. QUITE THE OPPOSITE!

There is nothing in Scripture to indicate that God's Spirit can be frightened off like a nervous dove. I get quite the opposite impression. It is obvious that there were shameful faults in the Corinthian church, yet Paul wrote to them:

> I always thank God for you because of his grace given you in Christ Jesus. For in him you have been enriched in

every way—in all your speaking and in all your knowledge—because our testimony about Christ was confirmed in you. Therefore you do not lack any spiritual gift as you eagerly wait for our Lord Jesus Christ to be revealed. He will keep you strong to the end, so that you will be blameless on the day of our Lord Jesus Christ (1 Cor. 1:4-8).

What is obvious as we read of the New Testament believers is their constant confidence that God is with them. Those first believers were not supersaints, yet they never seem to doubt that the power of God is indwelling them. They knew they were sinful and weak men and women, yet they grasped the truth of the love and grace of God. If modern Christians don't feel like that, it has nothing to do with their poor contrast with the Early Church. It has everything to do with perfectionist and legalistic teaching.

Congregations today are exhorted to strive for fitness, which is good. But such exhortations are often delivered in judgmental and censorious tones, producing a sense of spiritual inferiority among the people. Paul knew very well how faulty those first Christians were and he didn't hesitate to say so. Yet he stressed *what they were in Christ*. He left them with confidence in God, assuring them that God's Spirit was with them.

If you are baptized in the Holy Spirit, how long can you expect it to last? Forever? Or do you need to be "baptized" all over again every week or two? If the Holy Spirit "evaporates," can you say you are baptized in the Spirit anymore? The baptism in the Spirit means to receive the Holy Spirit, that you have begun a permanent relationship with the Spirit of God. *You are being filled with the Spirit as a continuous experience* (see Eph. 5:18). You only need to stay there. It is a simple matter of faith, not of high moral achievements. I think Paul asked a very relevant question in Galatians:

> This only I want to learn from you: Did you receive the Spirit by the works of the law, or by the hearing of faith? Are you so foolish? Having begun in the Spirit, are you now being made perfect by the flesh? (Gal. 3:2,3, *NKJV*).

It is a strange contradiction, which many have embraced, that they develop their spirituality by works of the flesh!

There have never been evangelistic successes in all history like those of the Pentecostal/charismatic believers of the past 100 years. What is their secret? The evangelists were absolutely confident that God was with them and their converts received the same objective assurance. They spoke with tongues and therefore *knew* they had received the Holy Spirit. The problem of whether they had or had not received the Spirit had for centuries worried the best Christians. Now they knew He was with them, permanently. It was *never* true that charismatic worshipers sought after tongues. They sought the Holy Spirit.

Note
1. Charismatic is a misnomer. They are actually not *charismatics* (gifted); they are *pneumatics* (filled with the Spirit). Tongues are a royal ensign at the masthead to show that the King is in residence.

A BLUEPRINT FOR EVANGELISM

As an architect provides his construction people with a blueprint for his building project, God has provided us with a blueprint as well. I am talking about methods and principles in evangelism. I want to make several observations on both methods and principles but will focus mainly on methods here. Then I want to look at Paul's great Bible discourse on the principles of evangelism. In the final part of this chapter I shall go back over the ground we have already covered and cultivate it a bit.

Biblical Methods and Principles

People debate the effectiveness of one method of evangelism as compared to another, method vs. method. Having traveled around the globe and witnessed many different methods in operation, I have come to realize there are many factors that need to be taken into account. Nonetheless, if there is one text in the whole of the Bible that provides the fundamental principle of evangelism, it is 1 Corinthians 9:22: "I have become all things to all men so that by all possible means I might save some."

PLANNING

They say that God uses men, not methods, but I don't believe God uses men who have no method. Whatever particular forms your evangelism might take, unless you have some sort of plan, your impact will be lessened or even lost.

FOLLOW-UP

When Jesus gave the disciples that second great haul of fish, they knew how many they had caught—153. There was no vague guesswork. Jesus said to them, "Bring some of the fish you have just caught" (John 21:10). The first time they went fishing according to Jesus' instructions they caught so many fish that their nets broke and the boats began to sink (see Luke 5:1-11). They were caught unprepared for the overwhelming goodness of God and could not cope. They were not organized for the scale on which Christ worked. The next time they were and they kept every fish.

When we win people for Christ, they must be kept and discipled, not readily allowed to slip back into the waters of the world: "Bring some of the fish which you have just caught." No matter how we evangelize, we make contacts, and at least formally, people go through the process of receiving Christ. Next they must be cared for.

PERSONAL CONTACT

Evangelizing is not a soulless business routine. When Paul went to Ephesus he got trouble from the business quarter—from the industrialists, especially the silversmiths. They were forging images of the goddess Diana and making an excellent living from their sale. The way it is put in Acts 19:26 is quite significant:

> This fellow Paul has convinced and led astray large numbers of people. . . . He says that man-made gods are no gods at all.

I expect that many of you reading this could check the Greek. I am told that a present participle is used here, so that the words "man-made gods" could be rendered "gods which are coming into being," signifying a continually dead operation—gods coming off the production line every day. That was the religion of these people—a depersonalized production line of religion, with every god the same.

That is exactly what Christianity is not. In our gospel meetings we want people to be born into a warm environment of love. Far more is needed than a signature on a dotted line. I like it when I see converts kneeling for an hour with someone praying with them, their arms around their shoulders, while the atmosphere of the stadium or church envelops them with worship and praise. New believers should not be stillborn. When a child is born, the first thing the doctor or midwife must do is to get the child breathing. A new convert should be quickly encouraged to make his or her first cry to God—get their spiritual lungs working in praise and testimony!

The gospel is a personal communication between people and their God. The present age is being dehumanized, with individuals being reduced to part of the traffic flow or to commercial units. In America you can do your banking, buy hot, cooked food, go to a movie or even attend a church service via television—all without having contact with a living soul. Service between human beings is being eliminated and turned over to robots. I look with horror upon some of the promised techno-logical "breakthroughs" which bring us closer to a life that is fully automated, imposing utter loneliness upon millions. People dread the stark loneliness of the cold, loveless, scientific future—it is as much a threat as the nuclear bomb. Evangelism is a heart-to-heart business.

Business methods are not a substitute for the gospel preached "by the Holy Spirit sent from heaven" (1 Pet. 1:12). Church-growth programs may be valid systems for applying business methods to church affairs, and if we can learn from business efficiency we should. After all, the Word tells us to "be diligent to present yourself approved to God" (2 Tim. 2:15, *NKJV*). Whatever methods we use, method needs power and power needs method. Both are means of communicating our dedication and love. The essential thing to remember is that God uses people, not methods.

In evangelism of any kind, our method should take into account that we are not dealing with machines or growing crops in a field, but we are working with human nature—and an unre-generate human nature at that. It means we must be flexible, adaptable and understanding. We are not pushing people through a sausage machine—sinners going in at one end and saints coming out the other. Every person before us is a unique individual, each with his or her own fears, hopes and reactions.

In our ministry we train counselors for our major gospel cam-paigns. Training is fine, but it is always hoped that they will be compassionate people with a listening ear. There must be meth-ods, but methods must be humanized; they must never lose the personal touch and never be rigid. The reason why God has so many different kinds of children is because He is a personal God and likes everyone to have personal attention from somebody.

Our Bible is our manual for people touching people. As we lay hands on those in need, in the name of Jesus, our arms become His arms, our love His love. The Church is Christ walking the streets again, showing compassion, touching the untouchable, not just "objectivizing a growth-area project." We weep with those who weep and rejoice with those who rejoice. Business talks about its "objectivized philosophy." But God's objectivized philosophy was expressed by the two arms of Christ stretched wide on the Cross, protecting mankind from the legions of hell.

YOUR INDIVIDUAL APPROACH

God knows exactly who you are and has a place specially made for you. You are you. If God has called you, then it is because you have a specific place in His plans. There is nobody else like you and nobody can take your place. If you don't do what God asks, nobody else can. Your fingerprint is intended to mark some area of the Kingdom and it is impossible to substitute someone else's print for yours. Working for God provides the opportunity to be what you truly are, allowing your true personality to emerge in service to God.

Each of us should do God's work in his or her particular way. I have a detailed blueprint for my own campaigns, but it suits my approach and my personality. We should at least consider the best way for us to be efficient in evangelism. What may be the best way for me is perhaps not the best way for you. But if you are doing anything for God, the first thing to realize is that it is *you* God wants to use, not a method.

LET THE METHOD FIT THE TASK

The first Christians found and developed their own methods. Jesus left His example, but no detailed blueprint for doing His work. The Holy Spirit will bless boldness and resourcefulness in the enterprise of the gospel.

Nowhere in Scripture is any one method for evangelism laid down. The early Christian workers made the most of every available opportunity. Scripture tells us what they did, but that does not mean their methods are now divine obligations for all that follow. There are, however, spiritual principles behind their activities and those we should carefully take note of.

God has given us brains, so we should use them to devise ways and means to get through to the masses of the unconverted of this age. This is not just number one on the agenda; it is what the agenda is ALL about. If every item, including "Other Business," does not relate directly or indirectly to evangelism, *then it has no business being on the agenda at all.*

Notice in the book of Acts that the disciples selected methods to fit the opportunity. Peter won the first converts on the Day of Pentecost, taking advantage of the opportunity presented by the crowd drawn by the disciples speaking with tongues. His sermon fit the occasion perfectly, explaining tongues and the resurrection with reference to the Scriptures. His sermon contains all the elements of the gospel; he simply communicated it using the present circumstances as his platform. Peter and the other disciples were so full of the gospel truth that they introduced it with natural ease at any time, any place, just as if they were talking about any other current news item.

KEEPING SIGHT OF THE ESSENTIAL

Every method should be soul-winning and not just church-filling. It is possible to fill a church almost anywhere. There are common attractions—music, drama, banquets, children's programs, costume occasions, anniversaries, Christmas, Easter, festivals, choirs, noted preachers, rock groups. New attractions will always be invented. But if the people do not hear the Word of God, any exercise becomes almost pointless. In the New Testament, no opportunity was missed. The whole idea was to find ways of bringing the Word of God to bear upon people's minds.

I have been saddened to hear of healing services that brought in nonbelievers but where there was no delivery of the salvation message at all, just singing and a call to come forward for healing. Some people apparently preach healing only, not salvation. *This is a neglect of both opportunity and responsibility.* The Lord said, "Preach the gospel and signs will follow." We must put first things first, the Word *then* the signs. Peter used a miracle healing in Acts 3 as an opportunity for evangelism. He followed the example of Jesus, who did the same. In fact, the whole book of John amply illustrates this pattern.

In Acts 4 Peter and John were arrested and brought before the authorities. As they faced the frowning faces of their interrogators, they turned their defense into aggressive evangelism. Stephen, the first Christian martyr, made the most of the opportunity to preach the Word, even as his enemies were poised to kill him (see Acts 7). The evangelist Philip conducted what we might call a "healing campaign" in Samaria, where Jesus Himself had prepared the way (see Acts 8). Paul went into synagogues, where there was an open opportunity to discuss Scripture. He simply got among the men there and expounded the Scripture readings.

Paul also took advantage of the schools of philosophy. Philosophers would often hold open court in the streets or other open-air meeting places, and Paul debated with them as he did in the school of Tyrannus (see Acts 19:9). In Athens he addressed the curiosity seekers "where they lived," as we say, quoting their own writers (see Acts 17:16-32). He took the gospel to kings and rulers in court and to people in prison with him, as well as on board a ship, where he spoke of his God when everybody aboard was terrified of shipwreck. If he couldn't be some particular place in person, he wrote letters.

CHURCH BUILDINGS

We don't know whether Christians possessed any church buildings in those early days. We know they did a little later, but neither Jesus nor, it would seem, any apostle ever preached in a Christian place of worship. They simply went where people normally gathered. Paul's first meeting in Europe was absolutely informal. It is recorded in Acts 16:13:

> On the Sabbath we went outside the city gate to the river, where we expected to find a place of prayer. We sat down and began to speak to the women who had gathered there.

For 20 years after Pentecost the Christians met in the Temple precincts. They were known as a sect of the Jewish religion. Samaritans would never have been saved if the apostles had merely invited them to the Temple to hear about Jesus. They wouldn't have been caught dead in that place! It was a national tradition to hate the Temple in Jerusalem, which is what set them apart from the Jews as a nation. The feeling of hatred between Jews and Samaritans was mutual. But Jesus crossed every traditional and social barrier and began a work in Samaria which others followed up later.

When we see the church building as the only place to win souls, this places a great restriction on our ability to witness. Churches cater to Christians, not to the godless. In Germany, for example, it is an embarrassing admission to say you go to church—almost as if you risked contracting the plague there. Going to church is considered dangerous, leading to mania or melancholia. Most Germans wouldn't be seen dead in church, and that is about the only time they *are* seen there! There is more chance of winning the football championship in an ice-hockey arena than there is of winning the German nation for Christ in church services.

> UNLIKE OUR MODERN MINISTERS, THE
> FIRST APOSTLES HAD ONE JOB ONLY: TO
> BRING THE KNOWLEDGE OF CHRIST TO
> EVERY MAN AND WOMAN EVERYWHERE.

The situation is perhaps even worse in the rest of Europe. In Great Britain, the law does not permit appeal for conversions to be made on television. Other strategies must be found to reach the lost.

REACHING THOSE WHO DON'T GO TO CHURCH

The Great Commission demands that we confront people with the gospel wherever we find them. The aim is inclusive—all nations and whole nations. The New Testament never envisaged "church evangelism," as churches did not exist then. The situation was very different.

Today a church pastor has become a cheap-rate psychiatrist and social welfare officer—counseling, officiating at weddings, burying the dead, blessing new babies and so on. No apostle ever functioned like a modern minister! The first apostles had one job only: to bring the knowledge of Christ to every man and woman everywhere.

One important consideration in gauging the success of ministry is the impact that preaching the gospel has upon a community or nation. The question for me in my early years as a missionary was whether God was satisfied that we worked hard and won a handful of souls every year. Somehow I could not accept that. Surely God knew some other way. I was frustrated. I went out with my accordion and preached to the people at the bus station. Then I tried to get outside the mission itself by organizing a Bible correspondence course, which enrolled 50,000 people. That would have been considered a successful venture by most standards. But we must judge our labors not by how flourishing we are, but by whether we are seeing a maximum impact on the society at large.

It is a challenge to me to see what some people are doing in this and other lands. They are studying the grassroots problems, finding out what gets across, how to meet resistance to the gospel, how to capture the interest of those who have seen and heard it all before and are still unmoved. If we apply our intelligence to anything at all, this is what we need to think about. Jesus said, "The people of this world are more shrewd in dealing with their own kind than are the people of the light" (Luke 16:8).

POPULAR APPEAL

Does Christianity tempt people? Most people can resist anything except temptation! Or has the bread of heaven been presented as an inedible and unpalatable item on the menu? True, there are many presentations which are anything but attractive. They might appeal to those with a masochistic streak, the sort of people who would join the French Foreign Legion or feel they deserve punishment! That kind of religion is not that of Christ, nor was it puritanical. Somehow the Puritans have gone down in history as straitlaced, joyless and humorless, when in actuality, they were very happy people.

The followers of Christ are in a procession of life with the Prince of Life at their head. They were once blind but now see, were lost and are now found, were dead but are alive, and they "follow the Lamb wherever He goes" (Rev. 14:4, *NKJV*). They follow in His wake like a bright river of light.

Sometimes my message is called a "populist gospel." I don't see this as a bad thing. The phrase populist gospel is used in contrast to ministry with an academic gloss. Let me say that with Jesus, "the common people heard Him gladly" (Mark 12:37, *NKJV*), and the common people are always the vast majority. Abraham Lincoln said, "The Lord prefers common-looking people. That is why he makes so many of them." There is no virtue in presenting Christianity in a framework of intellectualism and fine art unless it reaches people for Christ.

Unfortunately, many people mistake the elevated feelings induced by great art for the presence of God. They walk through a vaulted cathedral and say they feel the presence of God. In fact they would get the same feeling if the place were a museum, which is often all it really is. They sense the awe of the architecture, but God "does not dwell in temples made with hands" (Acts 7:48, *NKJV*). Not everybody likes fine art. Can only cultured people therefore be saved? Must we like Johann Sebastian Bach and Gregorian chants to qualify for entry into heaven? Paul said his objective was "by all means to save some" (1 Cor. 9:22, *NKJV*).

I think there is some confusion about this. The setting of the gospel is not the same thing as the gospel itself. The gospel can be preached by an archbishop in a cathedral or by a converted drug dealer in a tent. I don't think that in either case there is any warrant for changing its simplicity. People may hear better English and more stately prose from the archbishop, but that would be incidental. The gospel itself is the greatness, the power, the majesty and the wonder of God on any occasion. Paul said, "I am ready to preach the gospel to you who are in Rome also. For I am not ashamed of the gospel of Christ, for it is the power of God to salvation" (Rom. 1:15,16, *NKJV*). *The gospel is greatness in anybody's mouth.*

In Africa I preach the purest and most direct gospel I can possibly express, and it has the most extraordinary effects. It breaks upon people's hearts and minds with all the freshness of an ocean wave. I know no techniques, no crowd psychology, no tricks, and we water nothing down. I preach a gospel about heaven, hell, repentance, faith, sin and forgiveness.

Methods and Principles in 2 Corinthians

On the subject of serving the Lord, 2 Corinthians is a wonderful resource. Paul himself is facing problems with a church and with people who want to be somebody. This epistle comes as near as I would want to get to espousing actual practical methods and details.

> Therefore, since through God's mercy we have this ministry, we do not lose heart. Rather, we have renounced secret and shameful ways; we do not use deception, nor do we distort the word of God. On the contrary, by setting forth the truth plainly we commend ourselves to every man's conscience in the sight of God (2 Cor. 4:1,2).

Paul was always deeply conscious of the need for messengers of Christ to be examples of their own message. This is his concern in these two verses. He is dealing specifically with the personal qualities of God's messengers. The secret of evangelism lies in the man, not in some strange mystical operation of God. Paul expresses this idea in greater detail later in this letter (see 2 Cor. 6:3-13):

- He describes himself as having received mercy, which is the greatest reason of all for a man to evangelize; he wants to tell everybody about this wonderful gift of God.
- This experience means that he does not fall away or give up.
- It means he doesn't live a double life, preaching the gospel on the one hand and living a life with some secret shame on the other.
- He does not adulterate the Word of God. He is given the gospel to preach and that is what he preaches—not his own notions.
- By these means he has the approval of people's conscience, at least. They can tell that he is an honest man of God.

STUMBLING BLOCKS

More than anyone else, a pastor or evangelist can be a stumbling block and cause people to trip up and fall away. He is in a position to do great good or great damage.

The difference between a successful man and a less successful one—in business or in ministry—can be a small thing. But this small thing can generate affection or dislike, leading to cooperation or unwillingness to cooperate, motivation or demotivation, harmony or discord. I could list thousands of pastoral character traits that have driven people away from churches, quite apart from major issues, such as doctrine or moral failure.

What is the use of evangelism, which brings people in, if unthinking leaders drive them out again? "He who does not gather with Me scatters" (Luke 11:23, *NKJV*).

But Paul had an answer: love (see 1 Cor. 13). Love is the comprehensive safeguard and secret of wisdom. Many common faults among pastors are simply not possible where a Christian leader truly loves his people. Paul saw all manner of such things. His letters are an education in handling people and not repelling them.

COMMENDING OURSELVES

Paul unashamedly says, "As servants of God we commend ourselves in every way" (2 Cor. 6:4). We rightly say, "Self-praise is no recommendation" (see Prov. 27:2), but Paul is not blowing his own trumpet here or recommending that we do so. He is not commending himself with hyperbole or looking for some cheap publicity. Pretentious and exaggerated public relations cheapens the image of evangelism. Charles Spurgeon used to say that David killed a lion and a bear and said nothing about it, but some people have a victory march when they kill a mouse.

Instead of glittering accounts of his successes, Paul recommends himself by endurance. *Endurance is the number-one item on his résumé.* Paul bore troubles, hardship, distresses, beatings, imprisonments, riots, hard work, sleepless nights and hunger during his ministry (see 2 Cor. 6:5).

To "commend ourselves . . . in great endurance" (v. 4) is active, not passive. When troubles come, people seem to think it is very spiritual to sit down passively and grin and bear it. Paul did nothing of the sort. He found ways of translating endurance into activity, to make himself an advertisement for the keeping and upholding grace of God. Paul wrote his epistles to the Ephesians, Philippians and Colossians while imprisoned in Rome. When physical and mental trials came to him, he jumped up, welcomed them and made the most of them to the glory of God. He thought hardships to be opportunities to display the mighty working of God in his own life.

THE ELEMENTS OF TRUE MINISTRY

Paul describes the positive elements of true ministry in 2 Corinthians 6:6,7—displaying purity, understanding, patience, kindness, the presence of the Holy Spirit, sincere love, honest speech and the power of God, all the while handling no weapons except righteousness in both hands, which means no arrogance and no belligerence.

INDIFFERENCE TO PUBLIC OPINION

In verses 8-10 of the same chapter, Paul describes his indifference to all reactions from the public and officials toward his labors. Paul willingly judges himself. He does not accept flattery. He is honest with himself. He knows what he is and is not.

Paul is a self-critic. If he had a bad time in a city, he says so and doesn't pretend it was wonderful. He describes the truth about his work and about himself and then shows how the world takes an opposite view. But he carries on regardless, through both glory and dishonor. It is all one to him, whether the reports are bad or good. He is open and genuine but treated as an impostor; treated like a nobody and yet he was famous; treated as though he were finished yet still active; beaten but still not killed; thought to be sorry for himself yet always rejoicing; written off as poor yet continuing to make thousands (now millions) rich; as having nothing yet possessing everything.

True, Paul was *the* pioneer of all pioneers of the gospel. God chose him for that specific and glittering privilege, and he certainly provided us with a human role model of the servant of God. He went on to say to the Corinthians, "We have opened wide our hearts to you" (see v. 11). That seems to me to expose the secret of one of the greatest men who ever lived and served God. People tried to break his heart, but he fought back with hands full of help and healing.

If we are going to make an impression as witnesses, it won't be as professional, slick, self-sufficient people. We are not called to be witnesses of our brilliance or our correctness; we are to be the *Lord's* witnesses, reminding people of Jesus Himself, whose suffering on our behalf left the ultimate example for us to follow. As Peter said, we were like "sheep going astray, but have now returned to the Shepherd and Overseer of [our] souls" (1 Pet. 2:25, *NKJV*).

Perhaps one of the finest evangelism-training courses we could take would be to shut ourselves away for a day and lay each of Paul's items of recommendation from 2 Corinthians 6 alongside our own lives to see how our priorities stack up. Are we being true to ourselves and to our commission?

If we are true to ourselves, we will be true to God. That is the best method anyone can follow.

ACTION IN THE BOOK OF ACTS

We can look at blueprints, talk and even pray, but eventually we must act—just do it and evangelize. Smith Wigglesworth was on one occasion traveling by ship and, in his usual way, managed to promote what he stood for among the passengers. A clergyman disputed his go-ahead boldness, but Smith's reply was typically concise: "The Acts of the Apostles were written because the Apostles acted."

The book of Acts shows the Church in action. From it we can gain much wisdom as we ourselves go forth in boldness. That is why I would like to look at the Acts of the Apostles at some length over the next two chapters. Allow me to begin by making some basic observations about this magnificent book and the men who lived it.

How to Get Results

Simply put, if we will do what the apostles did, we will get what the apostles got. People today talk about the book of Acts as depicting the model revival, but it didn't all just *happen*. The disciples made it happen. They received the Holy Spirit in the Upper Room and went out on fire to set the world on fire.

They didn't need any additional experience other than giving themselves to prayer and the Word of God. They didn't stay in the Upper Room enjoying their experience and trying to prolong it. Nor did they keep coming back for more of the Holy Spirit. The Holy Spirit is not given for self-indulgence. The disciples went out full of His power and proclaimed the marvelous truth of what they had received. Then God did the same things everywhere. Peter said the new converts in Samaria received the same gift the apostles received at the beginning (see Acts 11:15-17).

Men of Action

The disciples did not just pray and sit around waiting for God to enter the "playing field" to convert the world on His own through direct contact with unbelievers. It was the disciples' job to make first contact. They went out into the world so that the Holy Spirit might go into the world. Mark 16:20 says, "The Lord worked with them." It does not say they went with the Lord. They went and He went along.

If we truly follow Jesus, He follows us. When and where the apostles moved, God moved also. Natural effort releases divine effort; the Spirit works where we work. Not all evangelism leads to revival, but there's never been a revival yet without evangelism. Man needs God's power and God needs manpower.

Making the Most of Methods

The apostolic methods were not written down in order to tell us exactly how to go about things—they are not sacrosanct or definitive rules and regulations. But what we can learn is that the apostles fitted evangelism to the circumstances and to the outlook of their times. We must do the same in our age of telecommunications and the Internet. People of the Internet age think differently from previous generations. The text of the Bible brings us the truth, but it is our job to communicate it—and communicate it effectively.

Lifestyles of the Spiritually Rich

Let's be honest, the apostles of Acts did things which we would *not* normally dream of doing today. For example, they cast lots to see who should replace Judas Iscariot as one of the Twelve (see Acts 1:23 26). I don't know of any denomination today that would dare follow this example. Imagine choosing a chairman or president by seeing who drew the short straw or by tossing a coin!

Also, in Jerusalem the believers pooled their wealth and enjoyed an equal standard of living. This didn't work very well, however, and was eventually abandoned. When Paul wanted to help Judean Christians, there were no pooled resources in other churches and He had to make a very strong appeal to Gentile churches for gifts. Communal sharing did not prevent Christian poverty in Judea. (It may even have caused it!) I know some Christians who are still trying to live along communal lines. They regard the Early Church's failed attempt as binding on us today. But the apostles never said that communal living was a God-given rule for all generations to come.

Some people imagine there was a divine order compelling Christians in a given city to form a single *organized* church center. But there were no organized church groups as we know them today. A church group with a membership role would have been regarded as a rebellious group.

When Paul wrote to a city church, it did not have a postal address. When Paul named a church, he was thinking simply of all the Christians within that area generally. They may be divided into groups named after one leader or another, as they were in Corinth. But Paul recognized them all as "the Church." Cities were very small by comparison with most cities today. Rome itself had a population of only one million, Jerusalem only 50,000. Groups met in houses, each with its own "elder." We have found in our gospel campaigns that Christians of different denominations within a city will come together as one to help us. Unity is not uniformity; in Scripture unity comprises variety.

A God of Variety

What men did is one thing, but what God did is another. In looking at the book of Acts, we see the principles of God's blessing in action. Acts records manifestations of the Holy Spirit. We can base our expectations today on what we read, since what God *has* done He will *always* do. He may do it in a different way from the way He did it the first time, just as Jesus healed the sick in many different ways. God is not a duplication machine. His Word is not like computer software—you put the disk in and the same thing appears every time. God brings changes, but does not change His character.

He is the God of variety. One can always tell an oak leaf from, say, a horse chestnut leaf, but God never makes two oak leaves the same. He does the same kind of thing, but never simply churns out an assembly line copy of what He has done before. He has unchanging objectives but pursues them by many roads. People pray "Lord, do it again," but He may have other ideas. God doesn't give encores or repeat performances. He is in the business of meeting each of us where we are, just as He met people 2,000 years before us.

The Role of Jesus

In my former book . . . I wrote about all that Jesus began to do and to teach (Acts 1:1).

Jesus had only begun to do the things Luke had written about in his Gospel. Luke here tells us that Jesus didn't stop doing them when He was taken into heaven. He must have continued working. Indeed, we have no grounds for saying He has ever stopped. He has departed this world in physical form but still carries on His work. We read His Word to find out what His work was like, then we look around and expect to see and experience it—and we do!

Jesus' absence from the earth is not the same as mine from Germany. He works with His servants wherever they are. His wonderful promise is "I am with you always, even to the end of the age" (Matt. 28:20, *NKJV*).

If Christ is continuing *His* work, then He must have the final say in whatever any of us does. He sends His servants to perform specific tasks. We are told, "Each man has his own gift from God" (1 Cor. 7:7). Nobody can be anything unless the Lord chooses him or her. Jesus said, "You did not choose Me, but I chose you and appointed you that you should go and bear fruit" (John 15:16, *NKJV*). He warns us, "Without Me you can do nothing" (John 15:5, *NKJV*). We can, of course, preach without Him—

and, unfortunately, all too many do—but our efforts will amount to nothing in the end.

Jesus said, "As long as it is day, we must do the work of him who sent me [that is, the Father]. Night is coming, when no one can work. While I am in the world, I am the light of the world" (John 9:4,5). The work of the Father was creation. He did not create in the darkness, but first said, "Let there be light" (Gen. 1:3). He even made the sun and moon in the light. Jesus takes this up as His example. He is the light of the world, and while the light shone miracles were possible. In John 9, for example, the blind man was made to see.

But the night was coming. Night would close in, and for three days Jesus would lie in the tomb. The light of the world seemed to be snuffed out in the darkness of the dusty sepulchre. Christ went into the night for us. He stepped through the veil of death into the eternal darkness of the pit. But He shed His light there forever.

At the beginning of his Gospel, John writes, "The light shines in the darkness, and the darkness did not comprehend it" (John 1:5, *NKJV*). I am told that John uses the word which is translated "comprehend" (Greek, *katalambano*) twice in relation to darkness. The second instance is in John 12:35 where we read, "Walk while you have the light, lest darkness come upon you" (*KJV*). John is saying that so long as you walk in the light, darkness cannot get the better of you.

Darkness cannot gain mastery over light. The darkness of hell and death could not swallow up the light from heaven. No amount of darkness can stop a candle burning. The death of Jesus extinguished both His teaching and His ministry of healing and deliverance. The disciples performed no healing miracles from the moment of Christ's arrest until the Holy Spirit came. Then the light shone again and they carried on the work of Jesus.

The Role of the Disciples

Those whom Jesus sends are His *empowered* agents. We read of occasions when Jesus sent His disciples out on missions to extend His own work. In Matthew 10:1 we read, "He called his twelve disciples to him and gave them authority to drive out evil spirits and to heal every disease and sickness." In Luke 10 He specifically instructed them to heal the sick, and then went on to say, "I have given you authority to trample on snakes and scorpions and to overcome all the power of the enemy" (v. 19). But when Jesus died and made only occasional resurrection appearances, they could apparently do nothing. When He sent the Holy Spirit at Pentecost, His work continued through them.

Today Jesus is physically absent from the world and the visible Church has become His Body. Believers have the power of attorney to act on His behalf in continuation of His ministry. They have His powerful resources and supplies at their disposal. We are His executives in whatever office to which He appoints us. His resources are there to equip us for the purpose of getting the job done. Thank God we do not have to go out unarmed and weak.

Jesus assures us, "Whatever you ask the Father in My name He will give you" (John 16:23, *NKJV*). This promise relates to the work of God. God promises attention to our call when we obey His call. We can ask whatever we want so long as it is in accordance with His will. His promise does not mean that God is waiting to take orders from us. He is not a waiter at our table or a kind of genie that we can call up by rubbing a magic lamp.

He does not promise to fill our wallets and bank accounts. He has never undertaken to make His servants rich, with rings on our fingers flashing as we drive our luxury cars. What we ask is *for the Kingdom*. Jesus said we should not focus on things, but on the Kingdom. Do not misunderstand me, material goodness is no more wrong for Christians than the sun and the rain, but material possessions have no eternal value. More important is the knowledge that "goodness and mercy shall follow me all the days of my life" (Ps. 23:6, *NKJV*). But goodness and mercy follow us only when we follow the Lord.

The Name of Jesus

We have been given power of attorney within the scope of whatever assignment Jesus delegates to us. We are authorized to act in His name, and we stand in that name (see John 14:14; 16:23,24). However, His name is not a formula which must be repeated every time we do something. Not that there is anything wrong in saying "In the name of Jesus"; we are only stating the basis for our authority. But we don't create power by it. We don't make our words miracle words in that way. We *have* power to do whatever He assigns us to do. Faith in the name of Jesus means faith in the person of Jesus, and that is enough.

That important spiritual principle is illustrated in the first apostolic healing described in Acts 3. Peter said, "In the name of Jesus Christ of Nazareth, walk" (v. 6). Later, Peter performs acts of divine healing using a different approach.

Peter healed a paralytic, saying, "Aeneas, Jesus Christ heals you. Get up." What happened? "Immediately Aeneas got up" (Acts 9:34). Jesus was clearly identified as the source of healing, but Peter did not resort to the formulaic "In the name of Jesus." Then he was shown Dorcas lying ready to be buried. He raised her from the dead without even mentioning the name of Jesus. First he knelt in prayer, and then "Turning toward the dead woman, he said 'Tabitha, get up!' She opened her eyes, and seeing Peter she sat up." The result? "Many people believed *in the*

Lord" (Acts 9:40,42, emphasis mine). The people believed in the Lord, not in Peter, even though Peter did not name the Lord when he raised Dorcas from the dead. The marks of Jesus are unmistakable.

Preach, Teach, Heal

The three commands of Christ are summed up as "Preach. Teach. Heal." The authority of Jesus covers both teaching and healing. We are sent to teach what Christ taught and to do what Christ did. We do it "in His name"; that is, as His authorized representatives. He taught and acted in the Father's name, and we teach and act in Jesus' name.

We sometimes heal in Jesus' name but preach in our own name. However *our* word is only our *opinion*. We are not sent to preach opinions. We declare His Word, not our word. Our authority rests in His authority. In Acts 4:2 we are told that the apostles "preached through Jesus the resurrection from the dead" (*KJV*). When they were arrested we read that the members of the council "called them and commanded them not to speak at all nor teach in the name of Jesus" (Acts 4:18, *NKJV*).

We should appreciate what preaching really is. Jesus went about "*teaching* in their synagogues, *preaching* the good news of the kingdom, and *healing* every disease and sickness among the people" (Matt. 4:23). What we call preaching—the Sunday sermon in church to a regular congregation—is what the Bible calls "teaching." *Bible preaching is not a sermon but a proclamation by a herald.*

As ambassadors we have no right to impose our own ideas upon people; we only have the right to announce what our King wants to say. The essential thing is that we are heralds with authority to proclaim the Word of God. Our job is to announce the truth of the gospel.

That again is the reason why Jesus said, "If . . . My words abide in you, you will ask what you desire, and it shall be done for you" (John 15:7, *NKJV*). If the gospel abides in us, then we can ask for what we want to proclaim it. If we want the power, patience, courage, strength and wisdom to do what He has called us to do, we can ask and receive.

> THUMPING AND SHOUTING DO NOT CREATE
> AUTHORITY. AUTHORITY RESTS ON FAITH
> IN THE WORD OF GOD AND THE AWARENESS
> OF HIS SPIRIT WITHIN US.

I have mentioned authority. Thumping and shouting do not create authority. I have no objection to signs of life! But authority is a hidden secret within our own hearts. We dare to make authoritative utterances because we are deeply convinced of their truth. This is not dogmatism but reliance upon the Holy Spirit to convince our hearers. Authority rests on faith in the Word of God and the conscious awareness of His Spirit within us.

Doing the Word

Everybody in the Church accepts that we must continue what Jesus began teaching, but we cannot just teach and omit what He *did*. We must heal as well as teach. If we don't then there is no real continuation of Christ's ministry. We have only completed half the task: "Go and make disciples . . . teaching them to obey everything I have commanded you" (Matt. 28:19).

We have not a hair's breadth of a warrant for splitting His teaching from His healing. They are mutually supportive. He taught by what He did and said, "If I do not do the works of my Father, do not believe me" (John 10:37, *NKJV*). The authority of His teaching rested on His miracles and His miracles on His teaching. If we teach what He taught, we shall do what He did, or our teaching becomes academic only. Jesus said, "[You] will do even greater things than these, because I am going to the Father" (John 14:12). Jesus spent half his time healing. To see his death as termination of that ministry is simply no credit to a changeless Christ.

That is how the Church becomes the manifestation of Christ again in a needy world. His compassion flows through our hearts and is seen in our eyes. It moves our feet as it moved His. Our hands become His hands and our voice His voice. Our arms of love are the only arms He has to use on earth. We can do nothing without Him and He will do nothing without us.

Living Truth

The gospel truth is living truth; it is not a collection of propositions. People talk about the "simple gospel message." It can be taken from half a dozen Bible texts. Each one tells us the same: You are a sinner. You are going to hell. Christ bore your sins. Believe. Receive forgiveness. Then you will go to heaven. All these statements are true. Other religions can compare their theories to it, but the gospel is not a formula or a creed or a set of formal statements and definitions. It is POWER.

Its proper expression has to be in works as well as words— and not *our* works only but the works of the Holy Spirit. To teach what Jesus taught we must do what Jesus did. If we preach a gospel in which there is no miracle, we emasculate the truth. James encourages us to be "doers of the word" (Jas. 1:22, *NKJV*) and John tells us not to love "with words or tongue but with actions and in truth" (1 John 3:18).

The epitome of moral and ethical teaching is the teaching of Jesus Christ. But without the miracle element it is dead. People talk about Christian principles but forget that Christ's greatest principle was that He came to bring the life of God into the world. They have missed the point. No amount of moral teaching could bring about the conversions we see today in the world—evil men, witch doctors, thieves, violent thugs. I absolutely *must* rely upon the miracle power of the Word of God. So far as healings are concerned, that is secondary to the mighty effect that the gospel has upon people's lives.

Christian morals and miracles go together. Without the revelation of an active God, ethics and morals are dead—just cold, mechanical legalisms. All of Christ's teaching was a warm, living revelation of the Father. Jesus said He always did those things which the Father did (see John 5:19), including healing. As the Father sent Jesus, Jesus sends us; it is a transferred mandate. Our work then isn't merely to tell people to be good and nice. We are to help them begin a relationship with Jesus, like the one He had with the Father—and the rest will flow from it.

More Than Intellect

The gospel is much more than an intellectual gospel. It provokes an inward effect, something very much like emotion—fire in the soul. We don't read the Bible properly when we read it unemotionally. The Word must be allowed to move us. Something speaks inside us and says, *This is true.*

Evangelism requires something more than academic knowledge. The gospel is not something you can learn as a statement to be memorized. It is not just information; it is the voice of truth amplified in your soul.

Christianity is not merely a statement of historical facts or a list of beliefs. Jesus is not just a historical figure. The gospel is a dynamic, life-giving force. It must be accepted by the inner man as well as by the intellect. Unless evangelism touches the heart it is useless, however accurate one's orthodoxy. The success of your message does not rest on logic. Christianity owes nothing to logic or to Greek philosophy. Christ's teaching slashes through the wisdom of this world—whether it's the wisdom of Aristotle, Plato, Buddha or Lao Tsu.

When Christian teachers of the past tried to demonstrate that Christianity was a rational system, they made a serious error. For one thing, their enemies treated the gospel the same way and tried to disprove it by reason. But Jesus didn't come to give us a rational system; He came to touch the springs of our life and to save us. People will never arrive at Christian belief by reason, but only by opening their hearts to His voice and to divine illumination. We believe what we believe because it is true, and it moves us and stirs us. Our beliefs are like music, the poetry of heaven which defies human logic. The gospel is love, pure love, and nothing is less reasonable than love. It has been called a form of madness, and yet it is love that makes the world go 'round, not logic.

Evangelism is nothing less than God loving people through us. The beginning of the Church was an outpouring of the Spirit who moved the apostles and moved the people who heard Peter preaching. The only facts these people knew were that they had crucified Jesus seven weeks earlier and were being accused of His murder. Peter had been with Jesus. He adored Him, imitated Him and had picked up His accent, or so I would believe. But one thing seems clear: Although He accused the crowd, he didn't provoke their anger. His tone was not hostile. He was not declaring war on them. Perhaps his words were reproachful. He spoke the truth but with the subtlety of love. These people had killed his best friend, but he told them that God forgave them and would wash away their sin.

I wonder why the crowd accepted the accusation of Peter and believed the story of Christ being exalted to the right hand of God. Just because Peter said so? Just like that? There were obviously forces at work. This was not mere dogma or loud assertions. Peter's words were like grappling hooks fastened into their souls. Christianity is a heart faith, not an intellectual process.

The Spirit of God interpreted the words of Peter for the hearts of his listeners. Peter declared that Jesus was risen and was made Lord and Christ, not the easiest concept to wrap a worldly mind around and grasp. All gospel preachers must rely upon the great Interpreter. It is no good *belaboring* your point and trying to *browbeat* the unconverted. If you do, it will sound to them as if you have a very weak case. *Argue,* and they will think it is all a matter of argument. Declare the truth without question as Peter did, and people are glad to find rest for their souls.

It is time to tell the world that our universe is not a scientific universe, that the laws of science tell only one side of the story. The world was made for love, by love, founded on love for the pleasure of the Son of God. Truth cannot be expressed through mathematics any more than a human being can. Knowing how old I am, how much I weigh and a few of my other vital statistics does not mean that you know me. The true me only flashes out from time to time in what I do. The truth is like that. One side of it may be examined by rational processes, in the laboratory or by chemistry and physics, but there's more to it. There is a nature in men and women which cannot be uncovered by the surgeon's scalpel. Our personalities respond to the power behind creation: the love of God. That is the way we are made and that is why the gospel impacts us profoundly.

A Gospel of Fire

They saw what seemed to be tongues of fire that separated and came to rest on each of them. All of them were filled with the Holy Spirit and began to speak in other tongues as the Spirit enabled them (Acts 2:3,4).

Fire! Ours is a gospel of fire. Fire in men and women means warmth, excitement, energy, zest. The disciples had a positive, living faith, plus a pulsating energy that made them want to go. They were neither possessed by God nor obsessed. But they burned with eagerness and love.

What has happened to modern Christianity? Why is it so cool and calculating, so sober and proper? During the age of reason, the age of tolerance, if people let their zeal show and spoke of their experiences with the Lord, their testimony was mocked as mere enthusiasm—they were slightly unbalanced; they had freaked out. The world could go crazy but the Church had to be dignified and sane. Church was no longer the place of fire. The people of God learned to show themselves rational and self-possessed. *But the world wants something to get excited about!*

Why should Christianity mean quietness, sleepy calm and mildness? Why do people talk about prayer as their "quiet time"? Prayer was no quiet time in the Acts of the Apostles! Twice, at least, prayer caused earthquakes. If you had been downstairs on the Day of Pentecost when the house began shaking, you would have demanded to know, "What on earth is that? What can they be doing up there?" They were just praying.

The world cannot understand what it is that swirls like a rushing wind and fire into our souls, but I am not going to oblige the world by stifling my joy. If they don't approve, then I say let them taste and see that the Lord is good (see Ps. 34:8).

9

ORDINARY MEN, EXTRAORDINARY MESSAGE

I think of the Bible with its lines of delicate print as being like a latticed window such as one might see in eastern countries. The Lord is standing behind that lattice, looking at us as we read. If we look closely we shall see His eyes between the lines. He is behind the Word of God.

By this time, I probably don't need to tell you that I am not writing an academic study; but this is not an apology. I have eagerly listened and gained what benefit I can from anyone who has a grasp of scholarly matters and I appreciate the value of their studies. But there is another side to understanding the things of God. There is such a thing as spiritual insight.

To restrict one's interest to the academic is to miss out on an aspect of godly life that is vital to the work of God. There are things to be said which may not be learned in a classroom, and I hear the Spirit saying, "He who has an ear, let him hear" (Rev. 2:7).

I trust that you will allow me to share with you certain things
I believe God is saying today through His Word.

Evangelism in the Early Church

As far as evangelism is concerned, the book of Acts is the key
book of the Bible, written to show how the disciples began to
carry out Christ's command to preach the gospel to *every* creature. Now what did that mean in those days? Well, they certainly didn't set up a tent and advertise in the press or on television!
Let's take a look at just what Jesus had engaged them to do.

The Message

Remember, the Early Church was venturing to do something
nobody had ever done since the world began: evangelize. The
Greek word *evangel* means good news, and the disciples turned
their good news into a way of life. They pioneered a concept
which launched and built the worldwide Church. They were not
only the first missionaries but also the inventors of missions.

Nobody before had ever had a god worth talking about or
worthy of being introduced to other nations. People's idol gods
were mostly a liability, more like troublesome parasites. Baal,
Apollo, Diana and others were not regarded with any kind of
affection. They were thought of as schizophrenic tyrants who had
to be pleased and placated. The authorities in a city would do
nothing without giving proper recognition to some god or other.
To fail to do so risked bringing deific vengeance down upon them.

The Messengers

The disciples were very ordinary men. Who were they really? You
could say they were nobodies. In fact, they were just anybody.

What Jesus did with them He could have done with anyone—even you or me. They were certainly not special; far from it. Jesus strolled along the beach and saw some local guys. He had met them before, but He chose them that morning, seemingly at random. Why not? It was not who they were; it was what He would make them. That's how it has always been.

We read that before Jesus appointed the 12 apostles He spent the night in prayer (see Luke 6:12). We are not told what or how He prayed, but it is always assumed He sought the Father's mind on which of His 70 or so disciples He should choose. I wonder if that was really the case? Did it take all night for God to give Him a dozen names? Did God give Him any names at all? Wouldn't anybody do if God empowered them? Or perhaps Jesus was again faced with a battle to choose God's way over that of human greatness. Was the temptation *not* to choose from this ragtag bunch, but to find wiser men, men of higher caliber and education, men of stature like Nicodemus, Joseph of Arimathea or some of the top rabbis? To stake the future of all Jesus had come to do on a bunch of raw, inexperienced young peasants is a staggering thought!

Even when Jesus was arrested and crucified, the Twelve were no support to Him at all. They all forsook Him and fled—and Jesus left the Great Commission in the hands of people like that! The chief among them cursed and swore and denied he had any knowledge of Jesus of Nazareth!

Actually, when you read what they were like, you might well think that the whole project of spreading the message of Christian faith was doomed from the start. They knew nobody, had no connections. They were ignorant of the world, its politics and philosophy. The Greeks boasted of great learning. The Romans had immense power. What could a heterogeneous bunch, most of whom were peasants or local fishermen without an education, do to conquer that world? They didn't even speak with an acceptable accent. The odds were heavily stacked against them.

Jesus sent them out without money and told them not to take any. They let Him down when it came crunch time. Even when He had risen from the dead He had to rebuke them for not believing what they saw with their own eyes. How could they make anyone else believe?

Yet they turned Jerusalem upside down and eventually the whole Roman Empire. Amazing! But such is possible with Jesus. His strength is perfected in our weakness. He brings to nothing things that are something by things which are nothing. God has chosen the disadvantaged to show that He is all in all.

The Lord loves to do things like that. Take the story of Gideon (see Judg. 6—8). Gideon demanded to know where the God of the Exodus was with all His mighty miracles. So God showed Him by overthrowing a vast army of Arabs, using three men who had no weapons at all—only torches, trumpets and pitchers! It isn't how big a man is that matters, but whether God has *all of him*.

The Undiluted Truth

The apostles were accused of changing ancient customs (see Acts 21:21), and that was indeed their intention. It was dangerous work. The famous philosopher Socrates had been sentenced to death for atheism—that is, for not believing in the gods. The apostles' work was to move a mountain—a mountain of traditions and attitudes, which over a thousand years had become the laws of nations. In fact, spreading the gospel went beyond changing ways and customs. They reshaped entire thought patterns of those times to penetrate the hearts, souls and minds of men and women. Twelve unlearned men. Imagine it!

Our work is not to make the gospel relevant to the world. Of course, we speak to the world in its own language. The whole idea of preaching the Word is to interpret it for the understanding of modern hearers. But the old liberal idea was to *adjust* the gospel to the pattern of the world to make it acceptable. If the world no longer believed in the supernatural, the solution was to preach a gospel devoid of the supernatural. This was a betrayal of the Christian message. We cannot compromise! To change the world we must be different from the world. We must challenge what people think. If they don't believe, we do not adjust to their unbelief.

The apostles preached Christ and Him crucified. Nothing could have been more calculated to ensure the failure of their mission. Crucifixion was for the worst criminals, the lowest of the low. Put a man on the cross and everybody mocked him. In no way was a crucified Jesus the ideal figure to appeal to either Jews or Gentiles. "He was despised and rejected" (Isa. 53:3). But that is the Jesus they knew and that is the *only* Jesus they preached. And by their preaching they conquered the world.

People must adjust to what God is. We don't preach a god made in their image. We must preach the Jesus of the Gospels— not some popular ideal but the Jesus of Calvary. If we preach Him as no more than a healer and a sweet, gentle, kind Jesus, then we have concealed the truth. We cannot allow our message to be influenced by public consensus, human notions or prejudice.

Jeremiah met plenty of popular prophets who prophesied smooth things that were nice for the people to hear, and he pronounced, "Woe to them" (see Jer. 23:1-31). People who won't face facts will learn the hard way. Jesus is the Jesus of the Bible. We can't reshape Him according to the ideals of the world.

John the Baptist, too, found the Christ to be different from Israel's popular expectations of the Messiah, but Jesus didn't change. It didn't matter whether He disappointed John, his own family or anybody else. He was what He was and His message to John was "Blessed is he who is not offended because of Me" (Matt. 11:6). We are not shapers or makers of the message. Paul said God had put him in charge of the gospel; he was its keeper, not its maker. We are only stewards of the truth, and it is required in a steward that he be found faithful (see 1 Cor. 4:2). The would-be Christ that has been popularly conceived cannot save us.

The Gospel Is Not Religion

The gospel abolished religion and introduced *Jesus*. The world had known conquerors who invaded foreign lands to plunder and kill their enemies, laying waste to vast areas. Others conquered with the intent of forcing native populations to adopt new habits and beliefs. But nobody had ever traveled to foreign lands at fearful risk just to love people, heal them, bless them and lift them out of their mess.

When Paul preached in Athens the locals said, "He seems to be advocating foreign gods" (Acts 17:18). But the apostles did not suggest a mere change of gods, i.e., Jesus instead of Diana. Jesus was not just a different, nicer god. To most Greeks, gods were just statues in the marketplace. People paid some homage to them and then forgot them. But the apostles were teaching nations about a God who had to be loved all day long and must never be forgotten. Christianity was a new way of life, not a few rites and ceremonies. Jesus was to be part of people's lives in a way the gods could never be.

The problem is that it is far easier to perform a rite or two before some image and then get on with life in one's own way. That was the sin of Israel, who had often forsaken the Lord

Himself. That is why the prophets said, "Remember the Lord your God" (see Neh. 4:14). The heathen forgot about their gods once they had paid them some small service, but the Lord was not to be treated like that. The absolute essence of biblical religion was summed up in the one great commandment: "You shall love the LORD your God with all your heart, with all your soul, and with all your mind" (Matt. 22:37, *NKJV*).

A Change in Values

Not only did Christian evangelism challenge the prevailing religious outlook, but it also challenged the existing system of moral values. The message of Christ was forgiveness, whereas the ancient world (and many cultures to this day) considered revenge a righteous thing. Christians spoke of hope as one of the three greatest qualities of life, but hope to the pagans was a weak sentiment of old women. The disciples saw bloodshed as a great evil, but the Roman and Hellenic worlds gloried in war and conquest.

The oldest literature in the world was that of Homer, who told stories of the Trojan War and its "glorious" slaughter. Homer's accounts of the terrible spirit of vengeance and bloodshed enthralled the Greeks and Romans, but such things became horrifying to followers of Christ. The Christian outlook would almost baffle the people of those cruel times. The apostles were subverting all common ideas of what was admirable and noble.

The world the disciples of Christ tackled was hopeless, but that did not put them off. *If they could do what they did, what can we do?* It is surely obvious that these simpleminded men could have achieved nothing unless they had the backing of God Himself. They were not promoting a religion that left people as they were, but a way of life that reversed everything people knew. The disciples were advocating a new world order with new kinds of people. And they succeeded. *That is the measure of the Power of God through the Holy Spirit.* That is what the gospel can do!

We owe thanks to the work of these pioneers who braved the darkness of a lost pagan world. They changed the world culture and made our job easier. They so deeply affected everything that we live in a different world than the one they faced. Jesus said, "I sent you to reap that for which you have not labored; others have labored, and you have entered into their labors" (John 4:38, *NKJV*). Those early evangelists laid the groundwork for us.

People today say they can live "decent" lives without religious belief. Perhaps so, but without Christian evangelism in the past nobody would know what a decent life is. The knowledge of Christ created decency, and our evangelism should at least keep that knowledge alive. Handguns have made it frightfully easy to slaughter our neighbors, but only the gospel can reintroduce mercy.

The Age of the Holy Spirit

The first disciples launched out to conquer the world with weapons that had never been seen before. They had secret forces behind them.

> We do not wage war as the world does. The weapons we fight with are not the weapons of the world. On the contrary, they have divine power to demolish strongholds (2 Cor. 10:3,4).

I have pointed out the vast spiritual change that took place with the coming of Christ. One of the first to realize this was a blind man whose sight had been restored by Jesus. He said, "Since the world began it has been unheard of that anyone opened the eyes of one who was born blind" (John 9:32, *NKJV*). He would also know that since the world began nobody had expelled demons or cured the deaf, the fevered, the lunatic and the crippled. Much more than that, nobody had come with a message that totally reversed cultural norms and transformed human personalities.

The age of the Holy Spirit had come. When Jesus sent the Holy Spirit into the world it was a cosmic event which could not be undone. It created a new order of possibilities beyond all that had been known since the days of Adam. A new form of life—resurrection life—was on tap. The apostles held the secret of this new life and they stepped out to demonstrate it—the first people in the world to do so. I think the Church is discovering their secret once again, as we are seeing the book of Acts extended into another century. Twice as many people have been converted during my lifetime than lived in the whole world at the time of the apostles.

Peter and John's first post-Resurrection miracle was the healing of a cripple, indicating the dimension of the resources available to them. That miracle was only a sign of greater things to come, as Jesus promised. The Holy Spirit had been sent to do much more than heal. I think that needs to be said. Healing is only one of the nine worship gifts named in 1 Corinthians 12. It is a very important blessing that we are to carry to a suffering world, *but* it is not the peak of the Holy Spirit's power. The sensational is not an accurate measure of the greatness of divine manifestation. The most spectacular occurrence may not be the greatest act of God. Nevertheless, when God heals, it is evidence of His power which has been made available to us.

When electricity was first discovered, it was considered by most observers to be an amusing novelty. Two hundred years ago, few people could conceive of the potential of the power of electricity to drive industry and light whole cities. When people speak with other tongues it is a sign of the potential of the power of the Holy Spirit. When Christ cast out demons by the finger of God, He said it demonstrated something greater, that the kingdom of God had come among them (see Luke 11:20). We can derive our confidence for what God can really do from any manifestation of the Spirit. The Spirit of God will not be limited to isolated incidents but will permeate our entire ministry, if we let Him.

THE SPIRIT OF GOD WILL PERMEATE OUR ENTIRE MINISTRY, IF WE LET HIM.

The greater works Christ promised included more than physical cures. The greatest thing was that the disciples were to be *witnesses*. The men of Athens called Paul a "babbler," but some of them were convinced of the truth of what he said and converted (see Acts 17:18-34). The witness of the apostles was supercharged, carrying conviction and working miracles of conversion.

Speaking the gospel message released the Spirit of God upon its hearers. The apostles were no longer just men; they were men of the Spirit, and it showed in more ways than just spectacular healings. When they prayed, things happened. When they were persecuted, they were able to rejoice. When they preached, they preached in power and in demonstration of the Spirit. When they touched the sick, they were cured. When they were troubled, they were not distressed. When they were perplexed, they were not in despair. If they were unsure, they were guided. If they were martyred, their blood fertilized the seed they had planted. If they were cast down, they were not destroyed.

The apostles were more than conquerors in all their conflicts and struggles (see Rom. 8:31-39).

These men outthought, outlived and outdied the pagans. They knew the source of true power. Paul said he was "strengthened with might through His Spirit in the inner man" (Eph. 3:16, *NKJV*). He became a minister "by the effective working of His power" (Eph. 3:7, *NKJV*). He said he was "strengthened with all might, according to His glorious power, for all patience and longsuffering with joy" (Col. 1:11, *NKJV*).

In fact, the apostles were a new species of *Homo sapiens*: spiritual men, the first on earth, new creations in Christ (see 2 Cor. 5:17). They were unaffected by the world's opposition in a way no man of the world ever could be. *And all that I have said about them holds true for thousands of God's servants around the world today.*

The same forces are available to every Christian today in the same measure as in the days of the apostles. However great our need, the power of God will be there to meet it. However great the demands of our ministry, the power of God will be there in sufficient measure. But note that there is no such thing as degrees of power—God does not tailor His power to match the degree of our supposed need. We have *all* power in Christ, all of us. The same resources are freely available to all who serve God.

The idea that we increase in power as we increase in prayer or holiness is not suggested anywhere in Scripture. The disciples were not a superelite holy group whom God equipped in a special way. They themselves encouraged us to know that the promise is to "all who are afar off" (Acts 2:39, *NKJV*). That's when I realize that I am mentioned in the Bible. I am one of those people "afar off." When we operate as the apostles did—in obedience, boldness and faith—then God operates. I have already quoted the words of Jesus: "Without Me you can do nothing"

(John 15:5, *NKJV*), but Paul gives us the inference "I can do all things through Christ who strengthens me" (Phil. 4:13, *NKJV*).

There is one gifting for every believer: We are all gifted to witness, but the gift comes with an obligation. We hear much about giftings. Many want miracle gifts, naturally. But the supreme gift already lies within every born-again Christian. It is Christ in us, the "indescribable gift" (2 Cor. 9:15), making each of us a witness.

As I have already pointed out, being a witness is about more than talking; the man or woman *is* the message. However, we must respond to the gifting. It is a poor way of conducting Kingdom business when a man has miracle gifts and does not preach the Cross. He is disguising the source of his power. Witnesses are witnesses to Christ's resurrection. We do not witness about any extraordinary abilities, special experiences or ourselves. We witness to Christ's death and resurrection—we have died to sin and live to righteousness by the life of Jesus. If Christ lives then we live and people should notice it sooner or later.

The World on Trial

When John and Peter and Paul went before the courts of law and Stephen before his accusers, there was little pleading for themselves and little argument about the gospel itself. They did not regard it as a controversial topic up for debate. They knew it was true and that was that. Their task was to announce it, and so they did. They planted the Kingdom's flag and unfurled the banner of the Cross. They came as ambassadors to a foreign power offering terms of peace. By standing firm they reversed roles and placed the earthly authorities on trial.

The kingdom of heaven is the superpower demanding surrender. Paul said to the wise men of Athens, "[God] now commands all men everywhere to repent" (Acts 17:30, *NKJV*). The early Christians presented the gospel as God confronting the world with its sin. So should we. It is not a choice, but the only alternative. The gospel brings the whole world before the judgment bar of Truth. Wherever they went, the disciples made judges and rulers feel as if they were up against it. This was so from the moment when Jesus stood before Pontius Pilate. Paul carried that air of truth with him so much that he could actually lift his manacled and chained arms and say to a king judging him, "King Agrippa, do you believe the prophets?" (Acts 26:27, *NKJV*). There are no apologetics when it comes to proclaiming the gospel. The gospel is simply to be declared; it will defend itself.

Sermons in the book of Acts carry little evidence of debate and controversy. They are assured, full of confident statements—a positive gospel. True, the phrase "defense of the gospel" is found in Philippians 1:7 and 17 (*NKJV*), but Paul was virtually a prisoner of war. He had come as an invader into the devil's territory from the kingdom of God. The only defense Paul put up was the positive gospel of Christ and Him crucified. He was not ashamed of it. He was never on the defensive, but always on the offensive.

God seeks no defenders. The whole idea is that He defends us. We can't turn around and say to God, "Lord, don't worry. I'm here. I'll protect You, never fear!" He hasn't got His back to the wall. He is not "poor old God"; His is not a dying cause. It is people who are dying, not God. Neither is God a "good cause." Men and women are God's good cause; He paid all He had for them. The best way to defend the gospel is to preach it.

Paul defended the gospel by taking the war into the enemy's camp. His defense was a good offense: the offense of the Cross. Prison was to him as good a place as any to bring the gospel. It was here that he could do the most damage to the prince of this world, like imprisoned Samson bringing the house down on his foes. Paul was not concerned with motivation or circumstance. There was a far more important consideration: "that in every way, whether from false motives or true, Christ is preached. And because of this I rejoice" (Phil. 1:18). And he encouraged other believers to adopt this position, "without being frightened in any way by those who oppose you" (v. 28).

It has been said that we are like advocates in court seeking to bring about a favorable verdict on Christ. But Christ is not on trial! He is the Judge. What people think about Him doesn't matter at all—except for their own sakes. Our approval or disapproval in no way affects Him. People who don't want to believe that God exists should be careful. Imagine if they were never to know He exists! Imagine all those unbelievers and doubters together in one place! I can't think of a worse hell than to be surrounded by people like that. A woman arguing about God once said to the great writer and historian Thomas Carlyle, "I accept the universe." He replied, "Madam, you had better!" I would rather have a difference of opinion with the 100 billion stars of the Milky Way than with its Creator.

What Can We Learn?

Acts chapter 10 is special because it records the conversion of the first Westerner, or, more precisely, a European—an Italian, as he would be called today. I am sure you know the story. Two men had a vision. One was in Caesarea and the other in Joppa. Cornelius, the Roman centurion in Caesarea, saw an angel. The angel told him to send for Peter, who would tell him how he and his household could be saved. Peter also had a vision that somebody would be sending for him. Both men acted on their visions.

Peter went to Caesarea and preached the gospel, and Cornelius and his household became the first European Christian converts. Let me make a few points about this:

PEOPLE NEED THE GOSPEL

Cornelius needed the gospel, even though he was as good a man as anybody in those days could hope to meet. He is described as devout, a God-fearer—a man who believed in the Jewish faith. He gave generously to charity and always prayed to God. In Acts 10:22 we are told that he was a just man who commanded great respect among the Jews. His alms and his prayers had caught God's attention. What is more, he carried his whole household with him in his godliness. Nevertheless, he needed Jesus.

I know that drug addicts, alcoholics, wife beaters and criminals need Jesus, but so do decent people, like the squeaky-clean youth and the war hero. When God sent an angel to tell a fine character like Cornelius that he needed to hear the gospel, we can draw only one conclusion: *Everybody* needs the gospel. And it's your task and mine to give it to them.

EVERY BORN-AGAIN CHRISTIAN IS CALLED BY THE LORD TO BE A FULL-TIME WITNESS. IT IS A GIFTING WE SHOULD NOT NEGLECT.

We cannot assume that people know the gospel when they don't. We have an undertaking with Christ to see that they do know. An upright life is no evidence of a saving knowledge of Jesus Christ. A sea of spiritual ignorance surrounds us. Advances in learning are indeed progress, but without faith in God increased knowledge results in a debit account. Knowledge only "puffs up," as the Bible tells us (1 Cor. 8:1).

The Lord has engaged us as partners to teach all nations and preach to every creature. *Every Christian should be taught personal evangelism as a specialist skill.* I am not talking here about training counselors for campaigns. I mean training people how to make cold contacts. Once shown how, every Christian could find it easy to introduce the gospel even to casual acquaintances. Every born-again person is called by the Lord to be a full-time witness. It is a gifting we should not neglect.

HUMAN BEINGS PROCLAIM THE GOSPEL

Back to Acts 10 and the story of Peter and Cornelius. You will notice that it was a human agent who was called to take the gospel to this European household. The angel said, "[Peter] will tell you words by which you and all your household will be saved" (Acts 11:14, *NKJV*). The angel presumably could have told Cornelius all about Jesus, but he said nothing. It is *our* job to take the gospel to people, not the work of angels. I would have thought angels would spread the word more effectively, but God in His wisdom has chosen to use His Church. Spreading the good news of Jesus Christ is our privilege, and God can dispose His privileges where and how He pleases.

God's plan for this world depends on human cooperation. One day we shall enjoy a righteous and sinless world and Christ shall reign forever and ever. The process has already begun. Angels could enforce righteousness and stop sinners in their tracks. They could arrive and convince the whole world of the reality of heaven and hell and judgment and God. But they don't do it. God has instead chosen the weak things of this world to confound the mighty (see 1 Cor. 1:27). Jesus could have called for twelve legions of angels to save Him from the cross (see Matt. 26:53), but the cross was the vehicle God had chosen to bring salvation to mankind. God wants people to be convicted of sin and turn to His Son for salvation, but by the power of love, not by forced faith or browbeating. If He used the "heavy hammer" method, He would achieve the right ends but by the wrong means.

THE POWER OF LOVE

Slowly but surely, love will conquer. The gospel is an expression of love. An evangelist is a channel of love—God loving people through him or her. Angels loving people would not be quite the same thing! It will be to God's glory that the battle was fought on the human level, led by a human Son of God.

We are not much in ourselves, just fragile centers of consciousness. If God failed to keep this planet at a fairly even temperature, people would soon vanish. Our intellects are limited. We are fallen creatures. Our characters are sin-spoiled and stained. We need to be saved. Nevertheless, humanity is the key to the Lord's divine plans—plans which stretch into the unknown vistas of eternity.

Through us God will put an end to evil and to the architect of evil, the devil. *Part of that ultimate victory is the present mandate to preach the gospel.* Indeed, it is the main part of the plan at present. Future plans are beyond our comprehension for the moment, but unless we uphold our part now, we will instead put a hold on God's wonderful schemes.

THE NEED FOR CROSS-CULTURAL EVANGELISM

Peter's conversion of Cornelius and his household was one of the first acts of cross-cultural evangelism. This was an extremely important development—something quite novel and astonishing in the world of that time. Between Peter's simple Jewish culture and the sophisticated affluence of a Roman official, the gulf in thinking was as wide as the Grand Canyon.

Normally, Jews never went into a Gentile home. But the Lord sent Peter a vision which helped change his strict Jewish mind-set, breaking down taboos and traditions (see Acts 10:10-17). Peter understood God's broader purpose, and so when the messengers arrived from Caesarea, he was prepared to go with them.

This special work of God in Peter's life pointed the way toward a world revolution—a new age in which racial differences counted for nothing except to make life richer. Peter had to adapt. Jesus did, as we read in Philippians:

> Being in very nature God . . . [He] made himself nothing, taking the very nature of a servant, being made in human likeness. And being found in appearance as a man, he humbled himself (Phil. 2:6-8).

God's servants must similarly identify with people wherever God sends them. When Ananias went to see the murderer of Christians, Saul of Damascus, who had been blinded by the glory light of Christ, Ananias addressed him as "Brother Saul" (Acts 9:17). This kind of reconciliation between men was an expression of what God was seeking to do for all mankind. It was one relatively small step for Ananias or for Peter, but a giant leap for mankind—a greater step even than when Neil Armstrong stepped down from the lunar module of Apollo 11 on July 20, 1969, to walk on the surface of the moon.

Hudson Taylor (1832–1905) was not the first missionary to China. But he arrived there to find Christian missionaries keeping up European appearances, living in European homes and dressing in European clothes. To the Chinese this looked like a foreign invasion. So, in order to gain acceptance with the people, Taylor adopted Chinese dress and styles. Paul's aim was similar:

> To the Jews I became like a Jew, to win the Jews. To those under the law I became like one under the law (though I myself am not under the law), so as to win those under the law. To the weak I became weak, to win the weak. I have become all things to all men so that by all possible means I might save some (1 Cor. 9:20,22).

Throughout Africa there are English-looking churches singing English hymns. Throughout Latin America there are American-looking churches singing American gospel songs. But things have recently begun to change. The people of these nations are creating their own churches with their own songs and the gospel is spreading like a bush fire.

It all tells the same story. When the purpose is to "by all means save some," the means of reaching that end are fully justified. The greatest force for change ever known did not set out to change cultures, but to drive the devil out of them.

THE MESSAGE IS ALL ABOUT JESUS

Let's take a closer look at the salvation message Peter had been sent to preach to Cornelius:

> I now realize how true it is that God does not show favoritism but accepts men from every nation who fear him and do what is right. You know the message God sent to the people of Israel, telling the good news of peace through Jesus Christ, who is Lord of all. You know what has happened throughout Judea, beginning in Galilee after the baptism that John preached—how God

anointed Jesus of Nazareth with the Holy Spirit and power, and how he went around doing good and healing all who were under the power of the devil, because God was with him.

We are witnesses of everything he did in the country of the Jews and in Jerusalem. They killed him by hanging him on a tree, but God raised him from the dead on the third day and caused him to be seen. He was not seen by all the people, but by witnesses whom God had already chosen—by us who ate and drank with him after he rose from the dead. He commanded us to preach to the people and to testify that he is the one whom God appointed as judge of the living and the dead. All the prophets testify about him that everyone who believes in him receives forgiveness of sins through his name (Acts 10:34-43).

No doubt, this is a summary of Peter's discourse, picking out the highlights, but we can see at once that Peter simply talked about Jesus. Politics, national relationships and social issues which agitated the people of those times were not even mentioned. Peter preached Jesus. He simply said that Jesus was Lord of all, which was—and still is—the true crux of every matter.

The business of comparative religions is really the business of contrast. There is little to dovetail. Take, for example, the founders of Islam and Buddhism. They professed to be no more than channels. Mohammed talked of his visions; Buddha talked of his enlightenment. Jesus did neither. He never claimed to be a prophet. *He said He was what they all prophesied about.* Christian truth is not a series of statements or a code of ethics or a program of religious observances. Jesus is the Truth. Christianity is Christ.

There is no need for us to attack Islam or any other religion.

There is no need to attack anybody's way of life, whether they live in the West, East, North or South. All we need to do is simply let people see for themselves what Jesus really is. As the Bible puts it, we need to encourage them to "taste and see that the LORD is good" (Ps. 34:8, *NKJV*). Jesus always wins the day. People can say nothing against Him. Nobody else saves, heals, expels devils and fills people with joy. And nobody can know what He is like until they meet Him.

Let me put it another way: Nobody stipulated what the Son of God should be like. Jesus is not the product of systematic theology. I know many say what they *think* God should be like and what He should do, but that is absurd. We might lay down standards for Miss World or Mr. Universe, but nobody can lay down standards for God or the Son of God. The scholars who write about the Jesus of history play that game. First, they produce their own model or ideal and then go through the Gospels, looking for pieces to make Jesus fit. Essentially, they produce their image of Him and then go to the Bible to see if He is there. For a century, scholars have looked for a socializing Jesus who didn't work miracles. They designed Him according to their rational, preconceived notions, but they have been unable to piece such a picture together convincingly, even after a hundred years of trying.

Jesus is too great for our small minds. He never fit anybody's pattern book, leaving the scholars of His day floundering and lost. The Queen of Sheba felt weak at the sight of the splendors of Solomon's lifestyle, saying, "The half was not told me" (1 Kings 10:7, *NKJV*). We don't call Jesus the Son of God because He measures up to what we think He should be. Any truth about Him is derived from Him, and His face outshines all.

I don't go to Africa with a book of doctrines. Evangelism there is easy if I stick close to the Book of books. My aim is to bring people into a personal and dynamic relationship with

Jesus Christ. That is all it takes: a presentation of the truth. The demons flee, sicknesses disappear, evil hearts are cleansed and witch doctors became saints.

In an earlier sermon, Peter said, "Nor is there salvation in any other" except in the name of Jesus Christ (Acts 4:12, *NKJV*). Well, until that statement is proved false, debate is pointless. If He saves, why turn elsewhere or even look to see what other people believe? Evander Holyfield and I could arrange a boxing match. Boxing analysts could find things the two of us have in common: Both of us are men; we have ears, feet and hands. But what's the point of all the prefight comparisons in the world if I can't measure up to his speed and power? And that's exactly the issue when it comes to Jesus! *No one can measure up to Him.*

Of course, you may find some kind of morals and ethics in Hinduism, but does Hinduism save? Can it give you forgiveness, joy and recovery? Has Hinduism, Islam or Buddhism got a Savior like Jesus, the Son of God? If not, any dialogue is a waste of time. Such a discussion would only deal with superficial issues and not with the thing that really matters. Unless there is another Christ, no debate is even possible.

Peter's sermon to Cornelius consisted of three major points:

1. A description of Christ's anointing of power to heal and deliver all who are oppressed by the devil.
2. Jesus was crucified.
3. Jesus rose again.

Then Peter concluded by drawing the meaning from those key facts: "All the prophets testify about him that everyone who believes in him receives forgiveness of sins through his name" (Acts 10:43). *If that message is not relevant to the world of this new millennium, I can't think what would be.*

Notice that the message from God was part and parcel of things that actually happened. It was not simply a collection of ideas, revelations, visions or enlightenment. The gospel is pragmatic. God has never dealt in mere philosophic concepts. He doesn't talk about abstract ideas of truth and goodness. He sent Jesus who was truth and goodness personified, so that we could see them for ourselves.

The first thing is to know Him yourself. Then you introduce Him to others. You can talk about Him as much as you like, and you will if you love Him. In fact, once you know Him you will not be able to keep quiet about Him!

THE GOSPEL AND SIN

One thing I have not yet talked about is *sin*. We cannot evangelize without facing the fact of sin. It is the basic tragedy of mankind, and that is why we do evangelize. After all, the whole world talks about little else. If nobody ever broke one of the Ten Commandments, there wouldn't be any news! The public appetite for news demands the spice of scandal in some form.

But to address the subject of sin and evangelism according to the Word of God, we must first understand the relationship between the Old Testament and the Gospels. The Old Testament molded the people who wrote the New Testament, and we must read the Gospels in the light of this fact.

The Old Testament and the Gospels

The Gospel of Mark begins:

The beginning of the gospel of Jesus Christ, the Son of God (Mark 1:1,2, *NKJV*).

It strikes me that this is a strange way to start a book. Nobody starts a book, an article or a sermon by saying, "This is the beginning." When you opened the cover of this book, for example, I'm sure you had no trouble locating the beginning of chapter 1. However, Mark was not simply stating the obvious or guiding dull-witted readers to the beginning of his book. What he was saying was that this is *the beginning of the gospel itself.*

Mark points to the Old Testament and begins to quote from the prophet Isaiah. His opening should be read like this without any full stop: "The beginning of the gospel . . . . as it is written in the prophets." The Old Testament and the revelation contained therein was, in fact, the beginning of the gospel.

Mark wants us to understand that the good news of Jesus Christ was not a sudden burst of Divine concern. It was always there—the prophets had leaked the news. What Mark says in his 16 chapters has its roots in the Scriptures as he knew them (i.e., the Old Testament). In his letter to the Romans, Paul tells us the same thing:

> Now to him who is able to establish you by my gospel and the proclamation of Jesus Christ, according to the revelation of the mystery hidden for long ages past, but now revealed and made known through the prophetic writings by the command of the eternal God, so that all nations might believe and obey him (Rom. 16:25,26).

This brings us to four things we need to know about the Gospel books as they relate to our mission to evangelize the world:

THE *GOSPELS* ARE THE FOUNTAINHEAD OF THE GOSPEL ITSELF

Unless we know the Gospels we don't know *the* gospel. We don't know what we are talking about without the four evangelists. A good salesman isn't just an auctioneer. He must know something about what he is selling. For anybody who is evangelizing, witnessing or teaching, the basic manual is the four Gospels.

THE GOSPELS INTRODUCE US TO JESUS, AND JESUS IS THE GOSPEL

The gospel is not just forgiveness or healing or how to make God appear and do things for us like Aladdin's genie. The gospel is not about what faith can do for you, but what *Jesus* can do for you.

I have observed that there is a mass of ministry by videos, tapes, books, etc., all concerned with the sensational and supernatural and aimed at creating faith for things to happen. Looking through a catalogue of audiotapes available from various international preachers, I noticed they are generally on one theme: the supernatural outworking of faith. But the early Christians sought nothing of the sort. They longed for holiness *and* to win the lost—and signs and wonders followed. They were not seeking power to impress or startle or to get attention. They were not seeking signs and sensations. Their interest was in the love of Jesus. Their aim was the glory of God and not personal gain or private advantage.

EVANGELISM IS THE PREACHING OF THE WORD, BY THE WORD

There are mountains of books, articles and sermons from Christian sources, but all too often they contain only what writers and preachers *think*; in these cases, such outpourings have little or nothing to do with the Bible. *We are to be ministers of the Word, not of moral reflections.* Many preach good things, interesting things, wise things and put together their own ideas and ideals but this can become a habit—one humans easily slip into.

To minister the Word means being daily under the influence of the Word, as with a familiar friend. This means, if possible, reacting naturally to the love of the Word. If you can cultivate discipline, study, meditation and concentration on the Word, that is an immense gain. Most people are not born that way, I know. But we can get help from those with this particular gifting; we can feed ourselves on what they provide and from it feed our sheep. By whatever means, somehow what we say must draw its life from the Word of God. Psalm 104:16 (*NKJV*) says, "The trees of the Lord are full of sap," not "sop"—mere stories or tear-jerkers. Illustrations should illustrate the Word, not merely entertain. It is the Word that converts.

THE WHOLE BIBLE IS THE GOSPEL

Our calling is to declare the whole counsel of God, not just a single concept we call the gospel. The gospel is often presented as a half dozen abstract ideas, complete with proof texts. But we are born again through the *whole* Word of God. Let's look at this scripture:

> Having been born again, not of corruptible seed but incorruptible, through the word of God which lives and abides forever, because "All flesh is as grass, and all the glory of man as the flower of the grass. The grass withers, and its flower falls away, but the word of the LORD endures forever." *Now this is the word which by the gospel* was preached to you (1 Pet. 1:23-25, *NKJV*, emphasis mine).

Peter is saying that the Word of God is the gospel. The *NIV* omits the key word: gospel. A literal translation is this: "What the Lord has said endures forever. What He has said is the message of the gospel that has been proclaimed to you" (*Word*

Commentary by Richard J. Bauckham). We should remember that for Peter, the Word of God was mainly the Old Testament, as the New Testament was only just being written. The Word of God is the gospel and the gospel is the Word of God. The terms are interchangeable. The gospel is not an extract from the Bible, but the whole Bible. *The four Gospels come to us wrapped in the pages of the Old Testament.* Our message to the godless world is therefore enshrined in the entire Word of God.[1]

The Fall and Rise of Man

Genesis 3:1-24 tells us of the fall of man. That is the link between the Old Testament and the Gospels: SIN. Any book on evangelism would be incomplete without a discussion of sin. The gospel I preach is that Jesus saves us from sin. I see sin all over the world deep-seated in human nature. It is like leprosy, a virus in the bloodstream. Wrongdoing is its ominous and ugly symptom. The symptom departs only when the disease goes.

I think of Naaman (see 2 Kings 5). He was a dignitary of Syria, but a diseased dignitary decorated with death. He came with his retinue of chariots and banners, glittering with military honors. But hidden underneath his uniform, he was contaminated with festering, leprous sores—a picture of the pomp of this world.

People admit to a failure here or a fault there. They may seek forgiveness for this or that. But that won't do it. That's like trying to cure leprosy with a bandage or two. We are not talking about one or two blemishes, but a legion of evils. The Old Testament teaches us that behind our sins is SIN—an instinct to sin which betrays us all (see Isa. 59:7,8, for example). Sin is a dark cloud neutralizing every good gift in our nature, a destructive bias. Many are used to confessing their sins and hearing absolution. My message is more than absolution. *It is deliverance!* Praise God! Salvation does not just hand you a clean slate; it opens prison doors!

Human nature carries the seed of its own ruin. Paul said, "When I want to do good, evil is right there with me" (Rom. 7:21). The Old Testament is the greatest exposure of human failure ever written. From Genesis to Malachi, it points to men and women and declares them to be fundamentally failures. The race of Adam is a fallen race. It shows it in all the tragedy and madness that is recorded from the Garden of Eden onward. "There is none who does good, no, not one" (Ps. 14:3, *NKJV*).

The gospel goes to the roots of the trouble. People sin because of what they are, so they need a change of nature. People don't just sin sometimes; they are sinners by inheritance. It is a *pedigree of imperfection.* Ill health, poverty, ignorance are evils but are merely derived. They are the bitter fruit of the root of sin. You won't solve the root problem by healing or education or the redistribution of wealth. We should do what we can to alleviate those problems, but the first thing to remember is that they come from what people *are.* Bad things don't just happen like fog at sea. We make them happen.

The trouble is we drive through life solo when our license does not permit it. Accidents occur as a result of bad driving, but bad driving happens because we drive without guidance, without a copilot. Many sit godless in the driver's seat of life, but the judgment of the court of heaven isn't just a few penalty points on our driving license. Jeremiah contemplated for a lifetime the whole nation of Israel carrying on without the Lord God, and he cried out, "I know, O LORD, that a man's life is not his own; it is not for man to direct his steps" (Jer. 10:23).

Strong's Concordance quotes more than 800 biblical references to the heart of man. Of these, 700 are in the Old Testament. Jeremiah 17:9 (*NKJV*) sums it up: "The heart is deceitful above all things, and desperately wicked." Sin is what we *are*. Our hearts are wrong. Jesus said that if the light of your eye is darkness, how great will be that darkness! (see Matt. 6:23). Mankind is spiritually astigmatic. What looks right isn't right. We have a warped view of existence without God.

GOVERNMENTS CAN PUNISH WRONGDOERS, BUT THEY CAN DO NOTHING TO ADDRESS OUR ROOT PROBLEM. SIN IS ONE VIRUS THE MEDICAL ESTABLISHMENT WILL NEVER ERADICATE.

The world carries on as if we are all really angelic beings who only slip occasionally. Our policy is to be good when it suits our own personal comfort or conscience. Governments can only legislate against errors and punish those who "slip" badly, but they can do nothing to address our root problem. Sin is endemic in human life. This is one virus the medical establishment will never eradicate.

Paul cried out, "Who will deliver me from this body of death? I thank God—through Jesus Christ our Lord" (Rom. 7:24,25, *NKJV*). An old hymn used to say, "I'm only a sinner saved by grace." I'm not quite in harmony singing that one. We are no longer *only* sinners. Believers are now children of God, redeemed, with a new nature that is averse to sin. We may sin, but we are not "sinners" anymore. We shall never have the angels in heaven whispering behind their hands as we pass along the golden pavement saying, "They look fine now, but you should have seen what they were. The Lord covers it all up, you know." We don't come before God as forgiven, but rather justified by faith, as having never sinned. We shall walk in white, in glory, in Christ.

"Whoever has been born of God does not sin, for His seed remains in him" (1 John 3:9, *NKJV*).

Stephen was martyred because he penetrated to the heart of human nature. He said that the root of the trouble, the cause of sinning, is resistance to God (see Acts 7:51). The religious rulers hated him for confronting them with that truth. We talk about people being demonized. We ought to have a word in English that means "sin-ized." Adam and Eve did not just eat the forbidden fruit; they had an agenda of independence and fled from the face of God. The devil's great cleverness was to send mankind on its way in self-dependence—gods in their own right. But the gospel goes for the devil's jugular:

- The gospel doesn't just change our ideas; it changes our hearts.
- The gospel is not the power of positive thinking.
- It is not just encouragement to act like children of God.
- It is not "all in the mind."
- It is not subjective, but objective.
- It is not a psychological adjustment, but a divine miracle.
- It is not a gospel of self-help, but a gospel for the helpless.

If we are to have truly Christian churches, they should be composed of people who have been *delivered*. The worst personality defect of all is pride in our self-sufficiency and goodness. This is godless *sin*. "All our righteous acts are like filthy rags" (Isa. 64:6).

Too often people join a church because it is all so good—nice people, nice music, good programs, activities for the children, crowds of friends, social gatherings, likable leaders, even faith for healing. All that is as it should be, but Christianity is primarily about the Savior. We can only come to God when this Savior has rescued us. Unless we turn over responsibility for our lives to Him, we shall be responsible on the judgment day for our own lives, our own sins and particularly the sin of rejecting Christ. To know Him we need to know His saving power. Sinners saved by the saving power of Christ comprise true churches.

Born-again believers may sin also, but there is a difference: They stay inside the family of God. John closes his first epistle with these words:

> If anyone sees his brother commit a sin that does not lead to death, he should pray and God will give him life. I refer to those whose sin does not lead to death. There is a sin that leads to death. I am not saying that he should pray about that (1 John 5:16).

What does he mean? John is talking about the difference between sinning when we are in Christ and the sin principle. He has explained this principle as that of anti-Christ, or denying the Lord. Sin is rebellion. Ephesians 2:2 describes humanity as the "children of disobedience" (*KJV*)—sons and daughters of the great world rebellion.

Until Christ came sins were covered, but there was a hard core of alienation that never changed. Christ's work was *reconciliation*. He made peace and reconciled the world to God at the Cross. He dealt with rebellion, made us His children and brought us back home. If a thief throws a stone through your window, he is a criminal. If your own boy does it, he is not a criminal. It reminds me of the story of the man in the prayer meeting. Week after week he relayed the same sentiments to God, always saying, "Lord, spring clean my life. Clear out the cobwebs." Finally one man had heard enough about the man's cobwebs and he called out, "Lord! Kill the spider!"

The godliest of the Old Testament people talked about forgiveness, but they knew their fundamental need was relationship with God. That is the genius of Hebrew religious understanding. The pagans never had the slightest conception of such a thing. Israel was more concerned about God being with them than with any superficial forgiveness for wrongdoing. The Lord was preparing them for the gospel. The Jewish people sought first of all that the face of God would not be turned from them. Once a year on the great Day of Atonement, the high priest went into God's presence (see Lev. 16:34). When he reappeared they gathered some assurance; it meant God was still in their midst.

That was but a shadow of good things to come (see Heb. 10:1). The reality came in the person of Christ. The Christian comes by a new and living way, boldly into His presence. Jesus said, "I am the way" (John 14:6). When the flesh of our Lord Jesus was torn upon the Cross, at the same moment the veil of the Temple in Jerusalem was violently ripped open (see Luke 23:45). The holy of holies lay open for anybody to enter. Jesus had made the true "at-one"-ment.

When we read the Old Testament, a man like David stands out as being ahead of his time. He grasped the fact that God was with him. This was a profound revelation and conviction. Few seemed to grasp it as he did. The Christian grasp of this is even greater. Christ not only forgives, but reconciles us to God. He brings not only forgiveness of sins, but He brings us back to God, brings us home and sheds the love of God abroad in our hearts by the Holy Spirit (see Rom. 5:5). Making us love what we hated and hate what we loved, He breaks down the walls which separate us from God. This glorious truth is totally outside the range of thought in every religion on earth except Christianity. It is unique. That is the gospel as it really is. It deals with SIN, not just sins.

Note

1. We can use Old Testament stories to illustrate the gospel, but that is not what was intended. Those stories and all we read there speak for themselves. Each contains its own theme, its own revelation of truth. These stories are not allegories of the truth, but each contains its own truth. We should not read back into it some New Testament thought, but rather it builds up to the truth in Christ.

EVANGELISM IN THE GOSPELS

In Jesus' supreme story of the prodigal son, the father not only forgave his son but also received him back into the family. He could have given the young man merely verbal assurance of pardon for his folly; he was not required to let the lad back over the doorstep. The father could have said, "I forgive you. Now you can go back to your pig farm. I will overlook what you have done." Instead he ran and kissed him. (The Greek tense of the word used in this passage means "kept on kissing him.") He brought his son home, clothed and fed him and reinstated him in his affections. *This is a breathtaking picture of what God is like.*

That assurance of the Father's love for us is also there in the Old Testament, but it only shines through pinholes. We have to look for it, but it is there from the beginning. In the New Testament, however, it becomes blazing truth. The sin principle withers: "Sin shall not have dominion over you" (Rom. 6:14,

NKJV). Not just this sin or that sin. We may even have a besetting sin, but it is rootless once Christ saves us. That is the gospel we take to the world.

How do I look at the four Gospels as an evangelist? They are God's revelation of His Son Jesus. There is no book in the world like them. They don't just give us the life story of Jesus. They are not biographies or histories. At least I don't see them that way. In fact, I believe they are books specially designed by the Holy Spirit for His own use. They are crafted to fit His hand like a cus-tom-fitted tool. He uses the Gospels as His means to show us what He wants us to know about Jesus. He can use other books and other means, but the Gospels are the fountainhead of what He reveals about the Son.

Miracles also witness to Christ, but we must find out first about *which* Christ. The Holy Spirit opens our minds to the true Son through the Gospels. He first gave us the Gospels and now gives us insight to see in them the glory of Christ.

The Gospel According to Matthew

The Gospel of Matthew presents two great, related themes: *the kingdom of God* and *the Lordship or authority of Christ Jesus.*

THE LORDSHIP OF JESUS

The essence of the message of the Early Church was "Jesus is Lord," and thousands died for daring to say so. What they preached is that Jesus *is* Lord *now*. He is not going to be crowned at some indefinite future time. He *is* Lord. Jesus Himself said, "All authority in heaven and on earth has been given to me" (Matt. 28:18).

We will never crown *Him*. The greater crowns the lesser, not the lesser the greater. He may enthrone *us*, but we could not place Him on the throne. We cannot choose Him as King. He is not democratically elected. He is on the throne by His own right as Creator. He alone is worthy. No one else is.

Evangelism is about proclaiming Jesus as Lord. He is able to save because He is Lord in every dimension, every sphere. The world resists, but in the end it must capitulate. Every knee shall bow and every tongue confess that Jesus Christ is Lord (see Phil. 2:10,11). This is the kind of language Paul uses when he talks about being ambassadors with a message of reconciliation (see 2 Cor. 5:18-20).

Jesus twice sent out disciples, first the Twelve (see Matt. 10:1) and then the Seventy (see Luke 10:1, *NKJV*), and through them He extended His earthly authority until their mission trips were completed. Later, on the Day of Pentecost, that extension of authority was renewed and became permanent.

Paul preached in Athens that He is Lord of heaven and earth. He commands all people everywhere to repent. For He has set a day when He will judge the world with justice by the Man He has appointed (see Acts 17: 24,30,31).

This is the burning truth of the first preachers of the gospel: Repent! Jesus is Lord, His kingdom is taking over the world and He is coming back to reign as Lord of all lords. "Kiss the Son, lest he be angry" (Ps. 2:12). Whether the world accepts Him as Lord or not, He *is* Lord.

THE KINGDOM OF GOD

Jesus gave Peter the keys of the Kingdom (see Matt. 16:19). This does not mean he carried the golden keys to the Pearly Gates, as many imagine! *The key to the Kingdom is the gospel.* "Except a man be born again" he cannot enter the kingdom of God (John 3:3, *KJV*).

Peter was not the only of us given the keys, but he was the first to use them on the Day of Pentecost (see Acts 2:14-41). He was also the first to use them to usher a European (Cornelius) into the Kingdom (see Acts 10:1-48). Peter flung the gates open to Jew and Gentile.

> And from the days of John the Baptist until now the kingdom of heaven suffers violence, and the violent take it by force. For all the prophets and the law prophesied until John (Matt. 11:12,13, *NKJV*).

I know this is considered a difficult verse, but one thing is clear: Until John the Baptist, the Kingdom was not present. John preached, saying, "Repent, for the kingdom of heaven is at hand!" (Matt. 3:2, *NKJV*), and Jesus began His ministry with the same message (see Matt. 4:17). The message of the Kingdom is the good news so often mentioned by Matthew. It was "new" news.

The gospel of the Kingdom is our message too, but the message has taken a new form since the events of Calvary and the Resurrection. We are children of the Kingdom proclaiming the need for submission to Christ as Lord and calling for repentance, so that all who do so may enter the Kingdom with all its riches and glories. We are not doctrine mongers. We are making an historical announcement, a proclamation. The gospel proclaims Christ as King!

As children of God, we live under a new Christ-centered order:

> [He] has qualified you to share in the inheritance of the saints in the kingdom of light. For he has rescued us from the dominion of darkness and brought us into the kingdom of the Son he loves (Col. 1:12,13).

The world is occupied territory in rebel hands. Once the whole world lived under satanic rule and oppression (see 1 John

5:19), but when Jesus entered the fray the forces of the kingdom of God began to assert themselves. For the first time demons were expelled by order as a sign of the kingdom authority in Christ. Now through His ultimate victory we are ousting the devil, proving we are more than conquerors through Him who loved us (see Rom. 8:37). Evangelism is spiritual warfare—every time we carry forth the gospel we push the forces of darkness farther into retreat.

Paul talks about the weapons of our warfare being the Word of God (see 2 Cor. 10:3-5; Eph. 6:17). To address the devil in prayer, praying against him in a kind of hand-to-hand combat, is unknown in Scripture. We have Paul's metaphor of putting on the whole armor of God, but every item—helmet, breastplate, shield, etc.—is *protective*, except the sword of the Spirit, which is the Word of God (see Eph. 6:11-17). We "wrestle" against these spiritual forces (Eph. 6:12, *NKJV*), but the Bible never says that prayer alone will win the day. Prayer has a vital place, but it is never designated as an active weapon.

We don't create our own power and authority by prayer. We have authority in Christ already, given to us through the victory of Jesus. We read in Revelation, "The accuser of our brothers . . . has been hurled down. They overcame him by the blood of the Lamb and by the word of their testimony" (Rev. 12:10,11). We shall overcome by the *word* of our testimony, not just our testimony. The word of our testimony is testimony *to* the active Word of God (see Heb. 4:12).

We come as servants of the King, who is Lord of heaven and earth. By the Word of God, anointed by the Spirit, we preach the gospel with authority, commanding repentance, our authority confirmed by signs and wonders. That is who an evangelist is; that is what he is appointed to do. Matthew provides us with the classic formula for fulfilling our Great Commission.

The Gospel According to Mark

Mark is the only one of the four Gospels which calls itself a Gospel. John never mentions the word at all. Matthew talks about "the good news of the kingdom" (Matt. 4:23), but Mark refers to "the gospel [or good news] about Jesus Christ, the Son of God" (Mark 1:1). The kingdom of God doesn't sound very personal; as a concept, it is quite impersonal and abstract. But that won't do for Mark. For him the good news is personal. It is about Jesus.

Mark's Gospel is a very personal one, despite the fact that the author was not an apostle and may never have met Jesus in the flesh. One of the Early Church writers said that Mark wrote down what he heard Peter say, and there is indeed much evidence that somebody behind Mark's Gospel observed Jesus at close quarters, someone who knew Jesus intimately. Mark uses words like "immediately" and "straightway" (*KJV*) quite often. That aspect of Jesus' ministry struck Peter. It would. Peter was an "immediate" person himself and noticed that Jesus didn't hang around, but got on with whatever had to be done. Of course, there was a difference between them: Peter was impulsive, whereas Jesus acted with perfect wisdom.

Matthew and Luke begin their books with talk about the birth of Jesus, and John talks about the Word "in the beginning" (John 1:1). Mark begins nothing like the others—no shepherds, no wise men, no angels. He quotes from the prophets Isaiah and Malachi.

We have seen already that the good news began in the Old Testament. The prophets generally spoke of troubles and evils befalling Israel, but in the midst of all the trouble Israel had brought upon itself there was good news:

"Comfort, yes, comfort My people!" says your God.
"Speak comfort to Jerusalem, and cry out to her, that her

warfare is ended, that her iniquity is pardoned; for she has received from the LORD'S hand double for all her sins."

The voice of one crying in the wilderness: "Prepare the way of the LORD. . . . The glory of the LORD shall be revealed, and all flesh shall see it together; for the mouth of the LORD has spoken" (Isa. 40:1-3,5, *NKJV*).

The good news is not some new teaching or some new gift, but a man—a voice proclaiming in the wilderness that we must prepare for the coming of the Lord Himself. The good news is personal: someone is coming! That's typical of God. He doesn't send ideas to people; He sends people. He sent Jesus and He sends *us*.

The gospel is a personal business, not just doctrines. To make Christians, we must get people attached to Jesus, not to certain evangelical teachings. Jesus said, "The one who comes to *Me* I will by no means cast out" (John 6:37, *NKJV*, emphasis mine). Christianity is a relationship, not a creed; so it follows that in our role as evangelists or witnesses, we as persons are important. Our personalities and Christ combine in this work.

John the Baptist was a prophet. He introduced Jesus. We may be ordinary people, but we do the same thing. That is evangelism, a matter of personality—men and women introducing the Man, Christ Jesus. Whatever media we use to communicate the gospel—radio, tapes, TV—somehow there has to be the personal touch. There can be a lot of the first-person pronoun "I" in what we say, because the Holy Spirit ministers through us to unveil the living Jesus.

Directness—a straightforward account of the truth in Christ—that is the spirit of a true evangelist. This spirit contrasts with the evangelistic style many people are familiar with—a fire-and-brimstone type pointing a menacing finger at his listeners and preaching *at* people. Mark has none of that. He tells the story and leaves it at that. Let the Spirit of God do His own work—we can't do it for Him. Our job is to proclaim the truth. When we ourselves know Jesus, our honest words will carry all the conviction that is needed. For the intransigent and those set in their hearts not to believe, debates and argumentation are useless. Let God take over. Some people have to travel a very rugged road to find the Lord.

To offer the gospel in terms of debate or argument can be self-defeating. Faith does not stand on logic or come by the wisdom of words. If we assert the truth and if we know the truth and if we know Jesus, then that will do. "A man convinced against his will is of the same opinion still," a proverb says. Mark's Gospel judges readers. If they are humble, open and receptive, they will believe. But those proud of their own intellects will not believe. They will demand proofs, which are not given except to the believer. Believe and you will see. If you won't believe, you would not see God if He opened the heavens and descended in front of you. In fact, that is what Jesus did! Through Mark, Peter shows us how to evangelize: Preach Christ, get to know Him, testify to Him being what the Word says He is.

Mark's Gospel has been called a "passion narrative with a prologue." The cross of Christ throws its shadow across half the book. Not much is said about the resurrection—only 14 verses. It is the Jesus who walked about Galilee and went to the cross that Peter remembers. Evangelism is a man talking about a Man he knows and loves—Jesus the Man and the Christ.

The Gospel According to Luke

The beginning of the book of Luke sets the general theme and tone. He begins with a quiet older couple, Zechariah and Elizabeth. They are considered deeply unfortunate because they have no children and they belong to the priestly tribe. For them to be without an heir would be a major sadness. But to announce the coming of His Son, God blessed this elderly couple with a most illustrious child, John the Baptist. Of him Jesus said that among those born of women there was no one greater than John (see Luke 7:28). My own impression about Luke is that he is concerned about deprived people and yet seems to focus quite a lot on wealthy and well-known people. He sees these people as *spiritually* deprived.

THE POOR RICH

Luke's good news is to those who have missed life, the outsiders, especially those who had the best of life in the eyes of most—people like Herod and the spiritual leaders of Israel. In Luke's second volume, the book of Acts, he continues in the same strain. Paul preaches to Felix and Agrippa and their royal courtiers and family, and a note of pity is there. Paul cries out, "I pray God that not only you but all who are listening to me today may become what I am, except for these chains" (Acts 26:29). It is almost the key theme of Luke and Acts: evangelism to the deprived rich.

The Gospel of Luke is full of examples. Jesus meets a man who has a dispute over an inheritance, money that belongs to him. Jesus shows him that money can be a curse and that he should look in a better direction for happiness, for "a man's life does not consist in the abundance of his possessions" (Luke 12:15). He talks about those who want to sit at the high table at banquets and points out that they could be happier sitting at a lower place (Luke 14:8-10). Jesus tells such stories as:

- The woman who has 10 coins but is in a state of near panic because she has lost one (see 15:8).
- The shepherd with a hundred sheep who is concerned about losing one (see 15:4).

- A father and two sons, all affected by possessions in some detrimental way: the prodigal who thinks money will bring him life; the other son who has everything but his heart is filthy and he refuses to join the merriment; the father whose money had brought him both the sorrow of losing the prodigal and the resentment of the elder son upon the prodigal's return (see 15:11-32).

Then there is the story of the beggar Lazarus and the rich man who passed by Lazarus each day. Both men die, but the rich man ends up in hell, pleading for assistance from Lazarus, who has gone to heaven (see 16:19-31).

Jesus shows concern for the "poor rich." More than a quarter of the references to poverty and the poor in the New Testament are found in Luke. The materially poor—people who have no money—are called "blessed," because their lot can be vastly richer than people of great wealth. Luke's Gospel contains the great poem-prophecy of Mary, the passage which we call the *Magnificat*:

> He has shown strength with His arm;
> He has scattered the proud in the imagination
>   of their hearts.
> He has put down the mighty from their thrones,
> And exalted the lowly.
> He has filled the hungry with good things,
> And the rich He has sent away empty
>   (Luke 1:51-53, *NKJV*).

In Luke 18:18-30 we are told of the rich young man who came to Jesus asking how to receive eternal life. That little episode ends with the rich man going away very sad. He kept his money, but did he lose his soul? Jesus commented that it was nearly impossible for a rich man to enter the kingdom of God—only by God's greatness could it be done. This calls to mind two verses in the book of Revelation. Here we find a stark contrast between poverty and prosperity:

> These are the words of him who is the First and the Last, who died and came to life again. I know your afflictions and your poverty—yet you are rich! (Rev. 2:8,9).

> You say, "I am rich; I have acquired wealth and do not need a thing." But you do not realize that you are wretched, pitiful, poor, blind and naked. I counsel you to buy from me gold refined in the fire, so that you can become rich (Rev. 3:17,18).

Christ in Nazareth declared His mission. He said, "The Spirit of the Lord is on me . . . to preach good news to the poor" (Luke 4:18). But who are the poor? James has much to say about that:

> The brother in humble circumstances ought to take pride in his high position. But the one who is rich should take pride in his low position. . . . The rich man will fade away even while he goes about his business (Jas. 1:9-11).

> God [has] chosen those who are poor in the eyes of the world to be rich in faith and to inherit the kingdom he promised those who love him (Jas. 2:5).

> James tells the rich to "weep and wail because of the misery that is coming upon you" (5:1).

THE GOD OF THOSE WHO DON'T BELONG

When Jesus preached in Nazareth, His hometown, His sermon was about two outsiders (see Luke 4:24-27): the widow woman who was fed during a famine in the days of Elijah (see 1 Kings 17:1-16) and the Syrian head of the armed forces who was cured of leprosy (see 2 Kings 5:1-14). God had met their needs, even though they did not belong to Israel.

Jews of Christ's day had little use for outsiders. Jesus' former neighbors flew into a furious rage at the idea that God would favor non-Jewish people and pass over His people in Israel. Luke uses this story to tell us that God is the God of those who don't belong. He comes to the lost ones, people drifting without an anchor.

Luke's Gospel is the book many have turned to in support of the "social gospel." Yet Luke really stands aside from issues of class and takes up the interests of those who for any reason feel they have missed life. For example, Luke 8:43-48 tells the story of the woman who touched Christ's robe and was healed of an issue of blood.

This woman's constant hemorrhage was a disaster. It left her anemic, weak, breathless and hardly able to walk about. She was also poor, having spent all she had on physicians. Because she had no money she was no longer able to eat nourishing food to compensate for her loss of strength. Also, she was ceremonially unclean, and because of her illness, everything and everybody she touched would be considered unclean (see Lev. 15:19-30). She had no friends and was unwanted—as much a social outcast as any leper.

Jesus made systematic circuits through the villages and she knew He would be coming. When He did, she struggled through the crowd and touched the fringe of His robe and was instantly healed. She felt it. So did Jesus. Now comes the point of the story, which was not so much the healing as what happened next.

He asked who touched Him. Well, dozens had. There would be the limelight people who would also be fussy and at the front, later boasting that they had rubbed shoulders with Jesus. Then there were the many other sick people who tagged along, hoping somehow to receive from Him a personal touch of healing. There was a constant rush of people who just wanted to be near to the miracle worker from Nazareth, but in that moment everybody stood still, Jesus looking 'round—almost as if He were accusing the one who had touched Him. The ring about Him widened, people backing away as His eyes searched the crowd.

Then the woman came trembling and afraid. Why? Because she had touched Him and she knew her defilement had defiled Jesus. (Likewise, our defilement of sin defiled Him—He was made sin for us [see 2 Cor. 5:21] on the cross.) All eyes were upon her. The whole crowd was quiet, everybody straining to see who had brought the party to a screeching halt. Jesus Christ, the Son of God, was entirely focused on one outcast, a little scrap of unknown humanity. Her loneliness and illness had put all heaven in a rage, and God sent His Son for her alone at this moment. Then came His verdict. The same One who will one day judge the nations and pronounce His verdict on mighty empires, the Lord and Maker of heaven and earth, paused for a moment and said, "Daughter, your faith has healed you. Go in peace" (Luke 8:48).

Whether we are rich or poor, great or small, Christ's eyes see each of us as we really are. "He did not need man's testimony about man, for he knew what was in a man" (John 2:25). His response to people was always the same: He loved them. Luke says He loved the rich young ruler. He loved John, one of the youngest of His disciples, a mere fisherman. People felt carried along with a wave of love by this Man, with His warm, outgoing, welcoming graciousness, His voice of throbbing concern. To meet Him was an unforgettable moment.

In Luke, we read that one Sabbath Jesus was walking through the cornfields. His disciples were hungry so they began to pick some ears of corn, rub them in their hands and eat the grain. When the Pharisees saw that the disciples were by definition harvesting—technically working—they said to Jesus, "Look! Your disciples are doing what is unlawful on the Sabbath" (see Luke 6:2). Luke tells us part of Christ's reply, but Matthew likes to quote Scripture and tells us that Jesus also said, "If you had known what these words mean, 'I desire mercy, not sacrifice,' you would not have condemned the innocent" (Matt. 12:7).

Jesus knew His disciples were hungry, but it was the Sabbath so they couldn't buy bread or make any. The Pharisees knew this too. But the Pharisees were not looking for human need—only human failure. They had no concern whether these men were hungry, but they had every concern for their rules and rituals. Jesus was teaching us to look first at our brother's need, rather than at his piety. Jesus is concerned with *people*, not religion.

JESUS IS CONCERNED WITH PEOPLE, NOT RELIGION.

He said to the Pharisees, "The Sabbath was made for man, not man for the Sabbath" (Mark 2:27). In fact, the law of the Sabbath was meant to be a law of liberty. As slaves in Egypt, the children of Israel had worked seven days a week. When they came out of slavery, God told the Israelites to rest one day a week. But through the centuries, the learned men of Israel had twisted the meaning of the Sabbath into a command to not do work, which had become more of a burden than the work itself! The Sabbath of rest had become a heavy load—one too heavy to carry.

But Jesus was the champion of the underdog. "He had compassion on [the people], because they were like sheep without a shepherd" (Mark 6:34). They had no one to champion them, but they flocked to Him because they knew He was strong enough for the job. The most memorable moment in our lives is the day and hour when Jesus comes into our hearts—as if we were the only ones. It is the day the world began for each of us, which of course is great stuff for the evangelists and for personal witnesses. Whether you are witnessing to one or one hundred thousand, Jesus saves on a one-to-one basis only. He works with individuals and every one is special. Each person He calls to Him has a key future role in the plans and purposes of God.

Luke 8:27-39 tells us about Jesus expelling a legion of demons from the demoniac and allowing them to go into a herd of pigs. The possessed pigs ran in a frenzy down into the sea and were lost.

> Those tending the pigs ran off and reported this in the town and countryside, and the people went out to see what had happened. When they came to Jesus, they saw the man who had been possessed by the legion of demons, sitting there, dressed and in his right mind; and they were afraid. The people began to plead with Jesus to leave their region (Mark 5:14,15,17).

Amazing! These men were afraid of sanity! People are afraid of true Christians in the same way, because they are too sane for this mad world. Of course, when the man was a raving lunatic they were afraid of his insanity. The world is always afraid, but Christians have no need to fear anything.

Strangely, the pig workers told everybody only what had happened to the pigs; nobody even mentioned the man. The swine were considered far more important than the victim of demon possession. He didn't count. When the people came they saw the man now delivered, sitting clothed and *compos mentis*. They were afraid, perhaps because they had plenty of other demon-possessed people among them at Gadera and if Jesus were to cast out more demons they may lose more pigs, so they asked him to go! But to Jesus this one man was worth all the pigs on earth. Pigs come a dozen to the litter, but each human being is a special creation, unique. There is joy in the presence of the angels over one sinner that repents (see Luke 15:7).

When Jesus rose from the dead, among the first words He uttered were not an echoing shout of triumph. It was just His voice, saying in the old way, "Mary!" (John 20:16). That is evangelism. Not ranting, rabble rousing, crowd psychology or stirring up mass hysteria, but Jesus putting His hand of love and healing and strength upon each one before us—and our manner as evangelists should suit what Jesus is doing. That is how I feel as I read the Gospels of the individual: Mark, with his personal touch, and Luke, with his concern over the faceless, the forgotten, the outsider. Evangelism brings in the lost and makes them part of the family.

The Gospel According to John

All Christian witness aims to do two things: to speak of things that are real and to demonstrate them. The more I read John's Gospel, the clearer those aims become. Preaching the gospel makes the gospel happen. The gospel is a news creator—you preach the good news and good news happens.

John talks a great deal about water, as we shall see. Water is described chemically as H_2O—two parts hydrogen and one part oxygen. Two gases. Mix them together in a container and all you get is gas. The gases are invisible and it is almost possible to believe they are not there. Many think that is all preaching is—talk, hot air, gas. We talk about things that unbelieving people cannot see and which they don't think of as being real.

Now apply an electric spark to your mixture of hydrogen and oxygen; the gases immediately explode and become water. The invisible becomes visible—real. That is how it happens with preaching. You can present the gospel truths, talking until you're blue in the face, but without the touch of the Holy Spirit, these glorious truths will remain hidden, unreal, incomprehensible to nonbelievers. The Holy Spirit provides the spark that ignites your words and the gospel suddenly becomes the water of life. But the gospel has no power to change lives until you preach it. Then, with an assist from the Spirit of God, the gospel becomes the power of God unto salvation.

John's Gospel tells of Jesus speaking to a woman who came to draw water from Jacob's well. Jesus said to her, "Whoever drinks the water I give him will never thirst. Indeed, the water I give him will become in him a spring of water welling up to eternal life" (John 4:14). *Real* water. Later, He told her that *real* worshipers would worship God in Spirit and in truth (see John 4:23,24). Jesus was contrasting the earthly with the spiritual, the symbol with the substance. Afterwards the townsfolk from her village said, "We know that this man *really* is the Savior of the world," or as the *RSV* puts it, "*truly* the Savior" (4:42, emphasis mine).

The notion of real or true things and the unseen reality behind them is found more than once in this chapter. The disciples had been to buy food and when they came back they asked Jesus to eat, but He said, "I have food to eat that you know nothing about.

My food is to do the will of him who sent me and to finish his work" (4:32,34).

He then talks about the harvest and uses the waving wheat field before them to symbolize the true harvest of souls (vv. 35,36). That is a very precious word for witnesses and evangelists everywhere. The true harvest! We have harvest thanksgiving in our churches, but in heaven the angels have thanksgiving whenever souls are reaped. We saw well over 100,000 people turn to Christ in Cotonou, Benin, recently—I suppose the angels had an all-night jamboree over that harvest!

John works on this theme of reality all the way through his Gospel. "The Word became flesh" (John 1:14, *NKJV*). The flesh was *actual* flesh—not a phantom—but the *true reality* was the Word. John wanted his readers to look beyond what their mortal eyes observe to glean the insight of the Spirit; but unless people are born again they cannot see. Only if they are born again can they see the Kingdom (see John 3:5). Suddenly it is there in all its wonder and thrilling hope and purpose! The reality beyond earthly appearances. John is always talking about the true light, true sight, true bread, true water, the true shepherd, the true vine—the real Truth.

Jesus said, "I am the way, the truth, and the life" (John 14:6, *NKJV*). Truth means reality, the genuine original. Jesus is the reality behind everything we see. He is the truth about creation, about the future, about us. John takes up the same theme in his epistles: "We have looked upon, and our hands have handled . . . the Word of life" (see 1 John 1:1, *NKJV*). The physical is the disguise for the eternal. John saw Jesus and every mystery was solved. Everything fell into place. Philosophy was finished.

John starts his Gospel with "In the beginning was the Word." Jesus is the reality from which *everything* came. At present science has hit a wall in their attempt to solve the problem of the origin of the universe. They talk with confidence about a Big Bang from which the universe exploded into being, but they have no idea whatsoever how that "thing" that exploded got there. What was it? Where did it come from? We know that however the universe came about, it came from God. Perhaps He began things that way: one unfathomable concentration of matter flung into the void by His almighty hand, exploding into the universe with all its wonder and diversity and energy and life.

> By faith we understand that the worlds were framed by the word of God, so that the things which are seen were not made of things which are visible (Heb. 11:3, *NKJV*).

In the Old Testament, we catch glimpses of an almighty God breaking in upon a dark heathen world, confronting and confounding kings, changing history—the God that answers by fire. We read there that God has created longings in people's hearts for reality, spiritual substance, something beyond and above and outside the everyday world with its ordinary events, science, reason and everything explicable. But the dimension of the Spirit is the world of excitement and satisfaction. *But how do we enter it?*

So we come to the crucial issue: *How do we make real things become real to our lost generation groping in darkness?* It is once again by the Word becoming flesh—the Word of God *in us*. The gospel in our lives, in our hearts and minds. Living people with the Living Word! Evangelism, which is all God asks of us. Declare His word and He will do the rest. Suddenly people will see.

The gospel is the bridge! It bridges the gulf between the earthly and the heavenly, this world and the other world, the mundane and the divine. Through it the power of God flows like an invisible electric current down an apparently unchanged and dead-looking cable. "We have this treasure in earthen vessels" (2 Cor. 4:7, *NKJV*).

We must build that gospel bridge with our witness. People walk across that miracle bridge into the light, into the Kingdom, out of condemnation into emancipation, into the house of the King, into glorious freedom as children of God. They that are blind shall see. The hungry will be fed on the true Bread. There is no other Bread that satisfies. There's no *ersatz*, no substitute, no alternative—only one Bread, one Water of Life, one Truth, all summed up in Jesus.

The way to experience the spiritual life is not by mysticism, transcendental meditation, fasting or deprivation. Spirituality does not come by sacraments or learning or suggestion of church architecture, music or poetry. You can only find it in the gospel, the Word of God. We are not preaching a *process* but a finished work, simply to be put into effect. There is no need to strive. Evangelism is not a desperate business. It is a joy!

We preach "not with persuasive words of human wisdom, but in demonstration of the Spirit and of power" (1 Cor. 2:4, *NKJV*). The gospel is a power pack, a life force. Preach it and watch it work! It's that simple.

EVANGELISM ACCORDING TO THE APOSTLE PAUL

In actuality, every word in the New Testament breathes evangelism. Even when Paul gives instructions to Timothy and Titus regarding the appointment of leaders in the churches, it is part of an overall evangelistic strategy. Let's now turn our attention to the apostolic letters to the Early Church.

The earliest of these letters is thought to be 1 Thessalonians. Paul and three companions had visited Thessalonica for only three weeks, during which time they were falsely accused, beaten, imprisoned, freed and urged to leave by authorities who were concerned that they would stir up a riot. Somehow in that brief time, many locals turned to Christ. The four pioneers had founded a flourishing church which proceeded to look after itself very well.

Preaching to a Pagan Society

Is it possible that the Thessalonians were aided in their efforts by their "religious" background as idol worshipers? Paul wrote to them:

> You turned to God from idols to serve the living and true God, and to wait for his Son from heaven, whom he raised from the dead—Jesus, who rescues us from the coming wrath (1 Thess. 1:9,10).   ˙

The gospel of Christ is the thought of God, not of man. Man never has and never will produce anything like it. We can preach it with pride. We can say like Paul, "I am not ashamed of the gospel" (Rom. 1:16). Nothing the former pagans once believed could have helped them to understand Christianity. They had to turn around and look in a whole new direction.

Liberals have suggested that pagan religion was fertile ground in which Christianity easily took root.[1] They like to attribute the rise of Christianity to Greek thought as much if not more than divine inspiration. But Christianity isn't like anything that had been thought of before. The gospel owes nothing to pagans, however great and wise they may have been. The early fathers of the Church made use of the ideas of the Greek philosophers to develop their teachings, but the true Word of God is original.

> The words of the LORD are flawless, like silver refined in a furnace of clay, purified seven times (Ps. 12:6).

Idol worshipers were required to change their entire thought patterns in order to follow Christ. They had to become new creatures (see 2 Cor. 5:17, *KJV*). The gospel matched nothing that was in their minds.[2] Pagan religions were woven into the official life of the city. Nothing was done without an offering to the gods. Any disrespect for a civic god might even carry the death penalty—a danger Christians had to take into account when preaching the Word. Multitudes of believers died because they would not offer a pinch of salt to the Emperor Diocletian to acknowledge him as "Lord and God." Pagan culture would have seemed impossible to change. The darkness stood defiantly against the light. Yet the early Christian pioneers prevailed. That is the power and glory of the gospel!

Now let's talk about reaching out in America. By comparison, sharing the gospel here can seem almost routine. Many conversions are the children of Christian parents and we thank God for such families. But there are the families who are almost completely ignorant of the Bible and live far from God. I am told that it is difficult to penetrate their world. But what about the world the apostles tackled? There wasn't a Christian in the whole of Europe or in most of the Roman world!

From the epistles written in those stressful times—many from prisons—we can look for guidance and inspiration. The Church was up against thousands of years of total heathenism which blanketed the whole earth, and Paul went into this almost alone. The obstacles were daunting, frightening. He said that he was in Corinth "in fear" and "in much trembling" (1 Cor. 2:3). But Paul stifled his feelings, or rather his passion for Christ overcame all other emotions (see 2 Cor. 5:14). He tackled the task, preached the gospel and the future of Europe was changed. The gospel proved equal to the problem.

That was pure evangelism, real face-to-face aggression for Christ. Jesus had been crucified, executed as a criminal, only 20 years earlier. That became the foundation of their message—a most unlikely way to impress the masses of the day. But the anointing upon the disciples' lives was made manifest in Thessalonica and large numbers of Greek idolaters turned to the living God. *This can be done today. It is still desperately needed!*

Target America

America is blessed. According to research, 50 to 60 percent of the population in this nation have religious interests of some kind. This represents great hope for the entire world. Praise God for it!

A religious tradition is a rich inheritance. Past generations have laid the foundation for a churchgoing people. Jesus said, "Others have labored, and you have entered into their labors" (John 4:38, *NKJV*). As a result, there is a reservoir of Christian interest ready and waiting to be tapped. It's an ocean compared to the small pond in Europe.

However, there's another, more disturbing side to this pluralistic country. Tens of millions in America are not interested in the things of God or are terribly interested in non-Christian spirituality; to reach people across this gap is a very difficult assignment. So, how are churches there growing? What about the megachurches? Are they making any dent in the number of the godless? Or are they really only organizing those who are already interested in Christ, rather than snatching brands from the fire (see Zech. 3:2, *NKJV*)?

These outsiders should be item number one on any church agenda, not just thought of under AOB—Any Other Business. If a church is doing well, gathering a large congregation, should it be satisfied? As long as there is a single unconverted person within reach, there can be no rest! A big church is not an end in itself. It is an instrument for world evangelism. If the church concerns itself only with its own affairs, its own membership, it becomes an efficient machine producing nothing but fine-looking leaves (see Mark 11:13). A church is not an institution but a vine branch meant to bear fruit. If the branch doesn't produce, it will eventually be pruned.

Churches can stimulate growth using good business methods, but only where there is a good market and low sales resistance, which seems to be the situation in North America. Now is the time to take advantage, to make hay while the sun shines. Commercial techniques merely exploit existing possibilities, but the gospel tackles impossibilities. True church growth comes by evangelism. "It pleased God through the foolishness of the message preached to save those who believe" (1 Cor. 1:21, *NKJV*).

A million people are reported to have come to one church in Florida last year and 180,000 responded to altar calls. That tells me there is an exciting and rising tide of spiritual interest. But what percentage of those who came had no interest in religion? How many were Christian sightseers coming because they heard miraculous things were happening there? Has this church fulfilled its purpose by becoming a big church? Being big, can it now rest on its laurels? Has the church done its job and fulfilled the Great Commission?

There is one thing I wish to interject here: I don't think the ultimate purpose of our ministry is to teach people how to get things from God. The aim of the Christian life is not get, get, get, but give, give, give. You may know of a version of Scripture called *The Message*. Allow me to quote its interpretation of a passage from Matthew:

The world is full of so-called prayer warriors who are prayer-ignorant. They're full of formulas and programs and advice, peddling techniques for getting what you want from God. Don't fall for that nonsense. This is your Father you are dealing with, and he knows better than you what you need (Matt. 6:7,8).

There is revival happening in China, but there the millions turning to Christ know very well that they are volunteering for trouble—possibly imprisonment—amid unrelenting disapproval by the government. Christianity is not a big, comfortable arm-chair and God is not on call to bring us whatever we ask. We are here to bring the world back to God.

Everyday Evangelism

The work of evangelism is to be continued even when there seems to be no revival brewing. The idea of evangelism itself often becomes confused with moments of great visible phenomena. Unless evangelism is linked with thrilling manifestations and tremendous spiritual trauma, some declare it to be a work of the flesh. Evangelism may not be revival as some see it, but neverthe-less it is the work God has set before us. It can be hard—a battle.

Evangelism does not always mean powerful emotions, revival fires, crowds, wonders, everything going great. The apos-tles' progress was not measured from revival to revival. Paul reg-ularly went into synagogues and would be thrown out after a row. Generally, their work was slow, building brick by brick. Paul described it like this:

In great endurance; in troubles, hardships and distress-es; in beatings, imprisonments and riots; in hard work, sleepless nights and hunger (2 Cor. 6:4,5).

It wasn't a relaxing picnic. This was war, enduring hardship as "a good soldier of Christ Jesus" (2 Tim. 2:3).

Returning to 1 Thessalonians, Paul speaks there of having "previously suffered and been insulted," but being "delighted" to share the gospel, with "toil and hardship," working "night and day," behaving in a "holy, righteous and blameless" manner, even as he was persecuted by his own countrymen (see 1 Thess. 2:2,8-10). In those days, such treatment was inevitable. For the privilege of preaching the gospel, you put your head upon the block for God. Paul says in 1 Thessalonians 3:3 (*NKJV*), "No one should be shaken by these afflictions; for you yourselves know that we are appointed to this."

Paul wrote to the Romans, "It has always been my ambition to preach the gospel where Christ was not known" (Rom. 15:20). Ways must be found to get to the unsaved or to attract them in bunches and then run a program just for them. In Europe they are using the Alpha course—meetings for nonchurched people only. And that is where the focus in Church affairs should be. Evangelism is the prior call of Christ and the last command He ever gave.

The apostle Paul picks up on this theme:

You know what kind of men we were among you for your sake. And you became followers of us and of the Lord . . . so that you became examples to all in Macedonia and Achaia who believe (1 Thess. 1:5-7, *NKJV*).

Followers of Paul became leaders of others. They took their cue from the work of Paul. For them, that was what Christianity was all about: telling others. Paul goes on to say:

In spite of severe suffering, you welcomed the message with the joy given by the Holy Spirit. The Lord's message

rang out from you not only in Macedonia and Achaia—
your faith in God has become known everywhere
(1 Thess. 1:6,8).

Paul adds that he would not need to come and bring the
gospel in that area, for they had already done it. How? By the
personal testimony of those who went against the idolatrous
tide in that great city. The authorities had seen to it that it was
not done by way of great public meetings. Instead, the winning
of souls was done using a one-to-one method, though it began
through the great evangelistic efforts of Paul. The two methods
are complementary.

But people must go to people. Mass campaigning and one-
to-one witness are part and parcel of the same commission. God
is the God of the individual, after all. He wants individuals to
receive individual attention from those who serve Him. In our
African campaigns we often preach the gospel to a hundred
thousand people at once, but we plan a one-to-one follow-up
contact.

Cold-calling individuals is not always easy, but a large-scale
campaign opens the door for individual contacts. Public evangelistic campaigns break the ice and give the personal workers a
background of strength. We try to plan that every person who
registers a response of some kind to the gospel call will meet
another Christian very soon after.

It is a wonderful thing to know that God plans to work by
using personalities—persons of every type bringing the gospel to
people of every type. Christ gave the same attention to an
immoral Samaritan woman as to the leading rabbi, Nicodemus,
though He gave no attention at all to Herod except to call him a
"fox" (Luke 13:32). The least and lowest must be listened to with
the same spiritual concern as if they were the presidents of the

U.S.A. and Germany or the queen of England. A lost soul is a tragedy whether he is a prince or a pauper.

Uncomfortable Christians

Our gospel did not come to you in word only, but also in power, and in the Holy Spirit and in much assurance (1 Thess. 1:5).

That's how it was done! Paul preached with power, though in human weakness. He declared Christ crucified, risen and coming again. He did not come demonstrating and boasting of the supernatural or trying to manipulate his listeners to emotional highs. Power is not for demonstration but for use; it is never on the loose. God is not in show business, and the Holy Spirit's power is not a novelty effect. It is the arm of God bending the gospel bow and shooting the arrow of conviction into the hearts of listeners.

OUR COOL, CASUAL,

LEAVE-IT-ALL-TO-GOD ATTITUDES

ARE ENTIRELY FOREIGN TO THE SPIRIT

OF THE NEW TESTAMENT.

Paul's comments in 1 Thessalonians are typical of the whole New Testament. Every apostolic letter is imbued with the same zeal and zest for the lost and for engagement in world expansion of the Church, winning every generation for Christ. That is what it is all about.

There are doctrines today that allow Christians to sit back and do nothing. They defend this cool, casual, leave-it-all-to-God attitude with Bible passages. They teach that God has settled beforehand that certain people are to be saved and that we can do nothing to sway His sovereign will. Well, I say emphatically that whatever texts people may quote, such an outlook is entirely foreign to the spirit of the New Testament. I don't fear contradiction on that point. The New Testament is vibrant with activity, and that activity is not about making Christians comfortable, but rather uncomfortable, until they carry the gospel to their neighbors.

Walking Revelations of Christ

[God] was pleased to reveal his Son in me so that I might preach him among the Gentiles (Gal. 1:15,16).

Christ lives in me. The life I live in the body, I live by faith in the Son of God, who loved me and gave himself for me (Gal. 2:20).

God sent the Spirit of his Son into our hearts (Gal. 4:6).

There is no way these words can be translated "God was pleased to reveal His Son *to* me." It is positively "in me" (Greek, *en emoi*). Paul is not speaking of what he saw on the road to Damascus, but what others see in his life. Once we meet Christ, then others can see Christ in us. Of course, the reason given that God was pleased to reveal Christ in Paul was "so that I might preach him among the Gentiles," the Gentiles being simply every race apart from the Jewish people.

The word "reveal" in that text is the Greek word *apocalupto*, from which we also derive the word "apocalypse." You and I are

God's revelations of Christ to the world. We cannot effectively convey Jesus on our own, so God does it for us. The life I live, I live by Christ in me. Otherwise evangelism would be an impossible ideal. What we are in Christ, we can't help being. I am German and have no difficulty in being German. If you have a gift it just shows. They say music, like murder, will out, and so will being a Christian. If His Son is in us, it is bound to show. More than that, the Bible says *God* reveals His Son *in* us. What we are, what we have, God takes up and makes something of.

If that is not evangelism I don't know what is—God revealing Christ in us that we might preach Him among the nations. The purpose is not to make people admire us as we strike an elegant Christian pose. The purpose is functional evangelism. Has it ever occurred to you that this is how Saul of Tarsus was saved? He watched a Christian die, Stephen, whose face was like an angel and who said, "Lay not this sin to their charge" (Acts 7:60, *KJV*). Nobody but nobody had ever talked like that in all history until Jesus.

Sure, there had been martyrs. The book of Maccabees describes the cruel deaths of a woman's seven sons, but they died defiant, not full of compassion for their persecutors. The law, after all, was vengeance: Treat an enemy as an enemy. Call upon God to curse him. But Stephen was a man who had the Spirit of Christ in him, shattering every known convention and praying for God to forgive his own vicious murderers, even as they ranted and raved and foamed in anger against him. That was new to Paul, and when Christ spoke to him on the Damascus road, the words of Stephen still troubled his conscience, amazing him.

That is the true way to bring the gospel to the world: Christ in us. Divine love is described in 1 Corinthians 13, but a better commentary is the life of Christ who loved us and gave Himself for us. That is how we show the love of God in Christ in us: we *give* ourselves. We can love people on our own, but that is only social love, charitableness, philanthropy. We have to possess divine love. Only the Spirit of Christ in us will make us outgoing self-givers, not in-takers. We must pour out our lives for the unconverted. Paul spoke of those who preach Christ in a spirit of contention (see Phil. 1:15,16, *KJV*); that is counterproductive, the truth given with one hand and taken away with the other by our envy and strife.

You know the old maxim, It is what you are, not what you say that counts. But what are you? That's the point. You are what is *in* you. Ezekiel 3:1-3 reads:

> And he said to me, "Son of man, eat what is before you, eat this scroll; then go and speak to the house of Israel." So I opened my mouth, and he gave me the scroll to eat. Then he said to me, "Son of man, eat this scroll I am giving you and fill your stomach with it." So I ate it, and it tasted as sweet as honey in my mouth.

The scroll was the Word of God. The Word should be in us. We are expressions of Christ, letters known and read by all men. Jesus was the Word made flesh. He was the living Word but the written word came alive in Christ, and so it should in us.

> Give us this day our daily bread (Matt. 6:11, *NKJV*).

Many scholars cannot seem to understand this portion of the Lord's Prayer. They debate the Greek while treating the bread as ordinary bread, not the True Bread. If you read this to mean the Word of God, there is no problem with the Greek or the English. There is daily Bread for us, *but it doesn't just come. We must ask for it each day.* Like Ezekiel we must open our mouths and

God will fill them. We shall get none unless He gives it to us. You might have the whole Bible committed to memory, but for it to sustain you as food it must be freshly given. And having received, you can give.

Let Us Make the Bridge Shake!

As God's fellow-workers we urge you not to receive God's grace in vain (2 Cor. 6:1, emphasis mine).

A friend told me that once when he was a three-year-old boy, his father was pushing a big two-wheel handcart loaded with wood and tools on his way to repair a house. His father sat the small boy on the cart, which his father was pushing. But after a while, the boy became restless and asked if he could push the cart. So, his father lifted him down. The bottom of the cart was actually higher than the boy's head, but he determinedly put his hands on one leg of the cart and they set off. Only now their progress was much slower as the father had to measure his steps to allow for the pace of his very small son. When they arrived at the house, his father told the owner, "My son has helped me push the handcart!" My friend felt very proud and pleased—indeed, quite important. But they would certainly have made the trip quicker if he had not "helped"!

God could do better without our "help." We probably hinder Him more than help, as Jesus said: "So you also, when you have done everything you were told to do, should say, 'We are unworthy servants; we have only done our duty'" (Luke 17:10). That is according to the *NIV*, but the original wording is that we are "unprofitable."

However, the fact is that God does depend on us. In this business of the gospel, He does nothing without us. That is the way He wants to have His great work accomplished. A tremendous evangelistic verse is Colossians 1:24:

> I rejoice in what was suffered for you, and I fill up in my flesh what is still lacking in regard to Christ's afflictions, for the sake of his body, which is the church. I have become its servant by the commission God gave me to present to you the word of God in its fullness.

Look at any building that perhaps expresses architectural brilliance. There the ideas of a human mind now stand like a symphony in stone, a vast work of art. Yet the designer likely never put a stone of it there.

The greatness of the church and the greatness of the gospel is the burning, living greatness of the heart and mind of God. However we can claim to help bring it to realization in the lives of people today. We can claim no share, no suggestion in its conception. The scheme seems simple enough now that it is revealed, but it was beyond human invention. No manmade religion ever hit upon it. But to bring it into effect in the world, there must be labor, or suffering, as Paul said. It can only be implemented by some laying down their lives. As Oswald Chambers suggests, we take our marching orders from Jesus Christ.

I heard a story from Africa. An ant sat behind an elephant's ear when the elephant walked over a shaky bridge. The ant said to the elephant, "My, didn't we make that bridge shake!" There's nothing that God and we cannot handle together. "For thine is the kingdom, and the power, and the glory" (Matt. 6:13, *KJV*), and ours is the labor, the prayer, the faithfulness, the courage, the sacrifice. One day we shall share His glory and enter into His joy.

Notes

1. They thought that the mystery religions contained ideas similar to Christian teaching, such as the new birth.
2. The mystery religions' rebirth was nothing like being born again of the Spirit. They talked about the soul, but they didn't mean at all what we mean. Their "soul" wasn't part of them. It was only a counterpart, a ghostly model or spirit-duplicate that existed in another world.

EVANGELISM AND SPIRITUALITY

People often confuse terms, thinking that evangelism and revival amount to the same thing. So it is with spirituality—the word produces different pictures in the minds of different people. And some teach that getting revival depends upon our spirituality—the indefinable depends upon the indefinable?!

Whatever you and I understand by the term "spiritual man," most everybody would agree that it includes the concept of obedience to God. Since evangelism and witness are commanded by the Lord, how can we develop spiritually without obedience to His command? Can we be spiritual and ignore the Great Commission? Some people say that the Church has to get itself right *before* it can launch out in evangelistic outreach. But launching out in evangelistic enterprise *is* getting the Church right. As we have seen, the Church exists to witness and the Holy Spirit is present in the Church primarily for that purpose.

Where a church concentrates its efforts and activities toward bringing in lost sheep, the quality of the church's spiritual life is enhanced. Evangelism has a sanctifying effect: Once church members catch the vision of winning converts, they become anxious to display true Christian qualities. Witnessing is therapeutic for what ails the church since churches that are winning souls can't afford to have divisions, troubles, gossip and so on. In the New Testament, spirituality is often related to the impressions we give to the outside world. In Matthew 5:16 (NKJV), for example, Jesus said, "That they may see your good works and glorify your Father in heaven." Peter echoes these words of Christ in his first letter: "Live such good lives among the pagans that, though they accuse you of doing wrong, they may see your good deeds and glorify God" (1 Pet. 2:12).

Unless a concerted evangelistic effort is made, a local church will not see many conversions. Without the fruits of evangelism, restlessness sets in. In the absence of new people responding to the gospel, there is talk about "something being spiritually wrong." A church that focuses upon itself and its members becomes increasingly introspective and mutual criticism tends to develop. When the number-one mission of the Christian Church is omitted from the agenda, somebody is going to be blamed.

Winning souls is not merely an end product of being spiritual; it is a way to become spiritual. To begin with, our prayers become urgent and objective, ceasing to be a vague "Lord bless me, bless this church." A focus on evangelism also calls for practical planning and plain hard work from everyone in the local body.

The Spirit and the Flesh

The adjective "spiritual" is applied to people only a few times in the New Testament, and in a couple of them, the reader senses a slight hint of irony. For example, in the midst of a rebuke to the church at Corinth, Paul writes, "If anyone thinks himself to be a prophet or spiritual" (1 Cor. 14:37, *NKJV*). Perhaps Paul had in mind people who claim with pride to be spiritual. As I said, people have their own ideas about what it means to be spiritual.

But in 1 Corinthians 2:15 (*RSV*), Paul writes, "The spiritual man judges all things." That helps. This was Paul's general teaching on living in the Spirit. In Galatians he contrasts the flesh and the Spirit. Paul provides us with a list of works of the flesh in Galatians 5:19:

> Sexual immorality, impurity and debauchery; idolatry and witchcraft; hatred, discord, jealousy, fits of rage, selfish ambition, dissension, factions and envy; drunkenness, orgies, and the like.

Yet in the same letter he also describes good works as being of the flesh, not able to achieve anything of eternal consequence:

> Are you so foolish? After beginning with the Spirit, are you now trying to attain your goal by human effort? Does God give you his Spirit and work miracles among you because you observe the law, or because you believe? (Gal. 3:3,5).

So just as sexual immorality and idolatry are works of the flesh, so are any efforts to be made perfect apart from faith! Many today seem to think they are saved by grace but sanctified by works. They act as though they believe that they have been saved by the power of God and yet must "earn" their way into heaven, being perfected without Him.

It is very difficult to define the spiritual man, because spirituality is an inner quality. Christian graces arise from an inner condition, although we can imitate such graces by human effort. Real fruit grows naturally on the branches; it isn't fastened on by hand. Man-made fruit is not fruit of the Spirit, however much like the original it may appear to be. Spirituality produces certain qualities, but those qualities do not produce spirituality.

Churches have their codes, written or unwritten, and indeed they should hold one another accountable (see Eph. 4:3-5,15-21). Members may naturally be expected to observe certain prohibitions: not going here, not doing certain things, not smoking, not drinking, not gambling, not swearing, etc. Such standards are fine. People should represent the church in a manner befitting Christ. But if standards like these have to be imposed on people as a matter of church discipline, then the whole idea of the work of the Spirit is lost. The church then is legalistic instead of spontaneous. The Galatians had adopted legalistic standards and were struggling. Paul warned them that to choose to live under the law—their law or any law—meant to fall from grace (see Gal. 5:4).

To Know Him Is to Live

Fleshly struggle doesn't make people spiritual. "Where the Spirit of the Lord is, there is liberty" (2 Cor. 3:17, *NKJV*). The children of God naturally manifest their divine nature. The Holy Spirit animates them. They are led of the Spirit, pray in the Spirit, walk in the Spirit, live in the Spirit, sing in the Spirit. Their happiness is not entangled with earthly fortunes and circumstance. When the issues of the kingdom of God are made paramount, then everything else falls into place.

> I eagerly expect and hope that I will in no way be ashamed, but will have sufficient courage so that now as always

Christ will be exalted in my body, whether by life or by
death. For to me, to live is Christ and to die is gain. . . . I
desire to depart and be with Christ (Phil. 1:20,21,23).

The apostle Paul wrote these words from prison where, in
his day, conditions were so bad that people wanted to die—and
many got their wish. But Paul was different. He embraced every
circumstance as being from God. Other prisoners wanted nothing more than release from the miseries of prison, even if by
death. Paul wanted nothing more than to be close to Christ, anywhere, in prison or out.

In the opening words of his letter to the Philippian believers,
Paul thanked God for his fellowship with them. But he also deeply
desired face-to-face fellowship with Christ, which was "better by
far" (1:23). However, Paul put the welfare of his brethren before
himself; he chose to remain among the living because it was necessary for his converts' "progress and joy in the faith" (v. 25).
Nevertheless, for himself all he really wanted was Christ. That
desire rose high above every passion of this great man.

We hear the same sigh from Paul later in the same letter:

I want to know Christ and the power of his resurrection
and the fellowship of sharing in his sufferings, becoming like him in his death, and so, somehow, to attain to
the resurrection from the dead. Not that I have already
obtained all this, or have already been made perfect, but
I press on to take hold of that for which Christ Jesus
took hold of me (Phil. 3:10-12).

Paul was the greatest of all evangelists. When Ananias was
sent to the street called Straight in Damascus to lay hands on
Paul, the Lord told him this:

This man is my chosen instrument to carry my name before the Gentiles and their kings and before the people of Israel. I will show him how much he must suffer for my name (Acts 9:15,16).

That was Paul's appointed work.

The book of Acts is largely a record of Paul's evangelistic career with Rome as its primary target. Christianity spread like wildfire in those early days following the Resurrection, though its history is mostly unrecorded. Acts is only a sketched outline of a divine strategy. The plan was for the gospel message to be heard by kings and rulers and eventually to reach the world's center, Rome. Paul was the burning arrow of God shot from His bow to penetrate that city. And Paul did it from deep inside the city—from prison—but he wounded the very heart of paganism.

Yet clear as his call was, in his heart Paul nursed a greater longing. His cry is heard again and again. For example:

Let us purify ourselves from everything that contaminates body and spirit, perfecting holiness out of reverence for God (2 Cor. 7:1).

Paul said his aim in life was "to take hold of that for which Christ Jesus took hold of me" (Phil. 3:12). Well, he was called as an evangelist and he had worked as no man ever worked. Yet he claimed he had not yet attained what God had for him. If Christ had taken hold of him just for evangelism, surely Paul had taken hold of that! He could not have done more. It is clear that Paul had something else in mind, a greater purpose beyond being an apostle or evangelist.

That greater aspiration was to know Christ. Although there is no end to knowing Him, Paul longed to go on knowing Him ever more deeply. Paul knew he had not reached the final depths. Certainly he knew Christ intimately, but God is an eternal objective. In fact, the apostle specified the only true way of knowing Christ was to be "exalted in my body, whether by life or by death" (Phil. 1:20). Paul wanted Christ's resurrection power life to be manifested in him more and more, then and there, before he died.

Paul aspired "somehow, to attain to the resurrection from the dead" (Phil. 3:11). That is a strange wish. Was Paul still in doubt whether he would be resurrected? Was he saying that he would have to work very hard to be included? No, he knew he would be raised from the dead in accordance with Christ's promise. In fact, Paul expressed that assurance in this same passage:

> We eagerly await . . . the Lord Jesus Christ, who, by the power that enables him to bring everything under his control, will transform our lowly bodies so that they will be like his glorious body (vv. 20,21).

The believer's eventual resurrection is one of the apostle's most constant and positive teachings.

What Paul was asking for in verse 11 was to increasingly experience Christ's resurrection power *now* in this life. He believed that what Christ had taken hold of him for was to enjoy resurrection life, which entailed more than being chosen to take the gospel to the Gentiles. Paul was no stranger to the resurrection life of Jesus—in Colossians 1:29, he testified to "all his energy, which so powerfully works in me"—and he knew from experience there were greater heights and depths, a fullness still to be reached. He had found waters to swim in and they had created within him a passion to explore the depths. To know and to go on getting to know Christ—that is life's highest prize.

In fact, that is why we evangelize. We are intent not only on saving souls from hell and getting them to heaven. We want to bring people within the resurrection dimension of Christ. We do not just preach a future promise of heaven, the better of two eternal addresses when we die. Although that in itself is a wonderful promise, we are talking about a new kind of life—physical and spiritual—that can be experienced in the here and now. A believer is a person who is no longer created for life on earth alone, but has been born again for life in the realm of the Spirit, the kingdom of God. That is the truly "spiritual man"—a new creation in Christ Jesus (see 2 Cor. 5:17).

When Paul talks about knowing Christ, he does not mean what we tend to think of when we say we know our friends. Friends encourage us; they help us. Friendship is precious. But to know Christ is to enjoy more than a handshake and a chat. Christ is to *live* in us. Some know Christ as a voice from the beyond; they know him mystically. But He is to be known *dynamically*. C. S. Lewis wrote about Christians as people who are "Christ-ized." Jesus identified with our human life so that we can identify with His divine life. Our aim is to be like Christ—not in behavior only, but sharing the inner qualities of His life. "Love, joy, peace, patience, kindness, goodness, faithfulness, gentleness and self-control" (Gal. 5:22,23) are external evidence of our internal experience.

Spirituality and the Power of the Holy Spirit

Spirituality, as Paul understood it, means power contact with the Resurrected One. Not a one-time experience but constantly flowing power. True spirituality is not the work of a moment—one abrupt miracle, a sudden avalanche of power. We don't *arrive* all at once. We are always on the way. Spirituality is a process. "Moment by moment I've life from above," goes the old hymn by D. H. Whittle. Another hymn, this one by Charles Wesley, says we are "changed from glory into glory till in heav'n we take our place."

I want to clear something up which seems to be at the bottom of much confusion in the Church. Holy Spirit power for witness is one thing, but you and I also need His power for our own personal spiritual benefit. Paul enjoyed power for service and power for his personal life. He wrote:

> We proclaim him, admonishing and teaching everyone with all wisdom. . . . To this end I labor, struggling with all his energy, which so powerfully works in me (Col. 1:28,29).

That was power for his ministry. But he also needed power to endure hardship and opposition and to rejoice in every affliction:

> Being strengthened with all power according to his glorious might so that you may have great endurance and patience (Col. 1:11).

We may have power to cast out demons yet fail to overcome the devil in our own hearts. That is where real spiritual warfare is conducted, not in the stratosphere. We can heal the sick and yet crumble at the first temptation placed in our path.

Paul described the signs of an apostle in 2 Corinthians 12. He referred not only to "signs, wonders and miracles" (v. 12), but also to bearing weaknesses, insults, hardships, persecutions and difficulties (see v. 10). Anybody can lay hands on the sick, and even children have preached the gospel. The prodigal son had the faith to claim and receive his inheritance but did not have the character to keep it. We need divine power for strength of character. True greatness endures, even when the whole world is in opposition to us. Only by the power of God are we able to overcome Satan when he engineers plots—both subtle and blatant—against us.

God has saved us in order to bless us, not just to make use of us. We are His children. We are not just convenient instruments to be picked up for a while and then dropped. God does not "utilize" us—He made us for love, not utility. He invites us to His banqueting chamber, not to a workshop. We are the Bride of Christ, not merely His kitchen staff. God doesn't intend for us to be workaholics, beasts of burden. He seats us among princes (see Ps. 113:8).

Paul encouraged his converts to reach out for others with the gospel, but he had another objective in view. In Colossians 2:6,7, he said, "Just as you received Christ Jesus as Lord, continue to live in him, rooted and built up in him, strengthened in the faith as you were taught." God wants to bless His people, giving them a taste of resurrection delights—freedom, relief, happiness. To work for God is a privilege, but that is not all there is to life in Christ. We should not be satisfied with just doing things.

When Jesus was ministering He found crowds waiting. The disciples told Him, "Everyone is looking for you!" He replied, "Let us go somewhere else—to the nearby villages—so I can preach there also. That is why I have come" (Mark 1:37,38). Jesus didn't burden Himself trying to do everything, grabbing every opportunity. He walked with God and left God to deal with the outcome.

We live in an age when "production" is a key word, and it afflicts the vision of the Christian Church—more work, more prayer, more activities, more new schemes. We like to be seen to be busy, not to get caught with our feet on the desk. Thus pastors are inundated, under pressure, their wives and families neglected. No wonder there are family breakdowns and divorces in the Church; so many husbands and wives have no time for one another. Somebody once parodied a famous biblical text: "I have come that they might have meetings, and have them more abundantly."

There is not a single suggestion in the New Testament that we should pray for power to do the work of God. After the disciples had waited 10 days and had received the Spirit on the Day of Pentecost, they went forth to witness. They had all the power needed—for always, unless they grieved or quenched the Spirit. They did continue to seek the Lord, but for their *own* spiritual progress. They were not looking to do greater things or work greater marvels, but simply to grow spiritually themselves.

Nobody who works for the Lord need lack power. The truth is, the limiting factor is the measure of our faith, not our virtues. Power rests on the degree of our faith, not our spirituality. So does revival. Some have written that power is given in direct proportion to the time spent in prayer. This is man-made theology. Jesus said, "The heathen . . . think that they shall be heard for their much speaking" (Matt. 6:7, *KJV*). Great faith and great spirituality are not always seen together. Jesus commended some people for their great faith who had no spirituality at all—including foreigners who had no knowledge of Christian truths or of the God of Israel. And it was by faith that they received great healings.

Holiness and Spirituality

Many Christians want to be used by God. They seek to live a perfect life to make them fit for service, assuming holiness will ensure success as a Christian worker—holiness as a means to an end. But holiness is an end in itself. Is our motive to be like Jesus or to be "something better"? Do you want to be like Jesus just so you can be a famous preacher? Christlikeness is not a mere step on the ladder of success. Christlikeness is the greatest success attainable! "Without holiness no one will see the Lord" (Heb. 12:14).

Service is not the greatest good. Holiness is greater—knowing Jesus. Christ gave us that lesson in the home of Lazarus. Martha was serving, preparing an elaborate meal for the Lord. Not an inch of unused tablecloth would show, in the usual eastern way. She imposed a duty on herself, hoping to please the Lord. But Jesus didn't want Martha to be His slave. He wanted her to know His love. Mary just sat with Christ, which pleased Him more than Martha's hustle and bustle. He said Mary had chosen the better part, which would not be taken from her (see Luke 10:42).

The Old Testament is brimming with men and women who did great things for God through His power, but few of them were notable as saints. We don't see too many churches called St. Jacob's, St. Moses' or St. Abraham's. Would any of these men be accepted into the ministry today? Suppose Moses applied for ministerial credentials with one of the denominations in America. Would he be approved? Remember, he had killed a man (see Exod. 2:11,12)!

David and Saul are an interesting study. Why did God use David and not Saul? He forgave David some awful sins, but He did not forgive Saul. Some people have a sneaking sympathy for King Saul. He was shown no favors. The prophet Samuel objected to Israel even having a king. For 50 years Samuel had judged the nation. When Saul was anointed as king, it meant Samuel was pushed out. He didn't agree with the idea of an earthly king for Israel and was pretty hard on Saul. Saul did fail but was shown no mercy—unlike David who sinned more grievously.

Saul was a big, rather lumbering type of countryman. He lacked the subtlety of David and was unschooled in the devious corridors of power. Saul became insanely jealous of David, but then to some extent that is perhaps understandable. Young David was pushy, foxy, brash and popular and Saul felt threatened from the start.

Saul was a moral man at least, which David certainly was not. Saul admitted he played the fool; King David did worse than play the fool. Saul never had to write a psalm like David's agonized confession in Psalm 51. Saul had a son, Jonathan, who surpassed in character all of David's treacherous sons. Saul was a peasant farmer. He did not adopt royal airs and graces and never built a palace or cultivated prestige like David.

God used David because he had an extraordinary faith. He understood God and thrust human understanding of God forward beyond his times. His very sin opened his eyes to divine greatness. The key was that he dared to believe God and acknowledge that the Lord was his King—the King of kings. God used this man David in the most extraordinary way. Even when David murdered a man, the Holy Spirit inspired him to write one of the greatest psalms of contrition ever penned. In fact, David's faith and work for God were most extraordinary for those remote days. Knowledge of God was little grasped; the prophets expounded it more fully much later. David advanced the faith of Israel to new heights and organized its entire system of worship. Though the character of David was very mixed, his effectiveness could be put down to one secret: his active faith.

Like David, many of God's great servants have been strange characters. Jonah ran away from God, taking off in a direction directly opposite to the command of God. He was the only disobedient prophet, yet he was the only prophet who ever brought a nation to repentance. Jeremiah and Isaiah were good men, but all their preaching never won one soul. Remember, Samson was a hopeless character. The Bible is a record of God's willingness to take up men and women whom we would consider unsuitable.

The apostles met a man casting out demons in Christ's name and told him to stop. But Jesus said they should let him continue (see Mark 9:38,39). The unknown man had found that faith in the name of Jesus did wonderful things. So have some today who do not appear to be great exemplars of Christian spirituality. For that matter, neither were the disciples themselves. But long before they became the saints we now seek to imitate, they cast out demons and healed the sick.

Recent events in America have shown that working miracles and building great works for God is no guarantee of anyone's personal virtue. That is why we must seek God to work in our own lives and not just for power to serve. We might have power to serve but be failures as followers of Christ. Ultimately, this undermines the Christian testimony. The sower treads the ground too hard to bear a harvest.

WE MUST SEEK GOD TO WORK IN OUR OWN LIVES. IF WE SERVE WITH POWER, YET ARE FAILURES AS FOLLOWERS OF CHRIST, THIS WILL SURELY UNDERMINE OUR TESTIMONY.

Jesus said there were those who on the day of judgment would call Him Lord and claim to have worked mighty wonders in His name, but that He would turn them away as "evildoers" (Matt. 7:23). I don't personally profess to understand how a worker of evil can cast out demons and heal the sick, but that is what Jesus said. This certainly shows that power of that kind does not come by holiness. Paul said that he wished to be found not in his own righteousness but in that which is by faith in Christ (see Phil. 3:9). God can work through us only by the provision of His grace and mercy; we stand before Him washed clean by the streams of the Savior's blood.

When I was a young pastor, I heard an old pastor praying. He spoke with regret of his serious failure. I remember praying at the time, "O Lord, grant that when I become as old as this man, I shall not have cause to pray that kind of prayer." The temptations with which we are faced in pursuing the work of God are subtle and almost compelling, but we desperately need to attain to holiness, to be quality Christian leaders and servants. I referred to Samuel earlier. He was a leader of flawless integrity, yet he was not perfect. He seemed to have it in for Saul and was quite merciless toward him. Yet he challenged the whole nation of Israel at the end of his life to find any corruption in him. Samuel had never enriched himself by bribery or misuse of power. Samuel was one of history's greatest.

True, we need not wait a lifetime to become perfect in Christian virtue before we can be of use to God. But for our own souls' sake, we should pray as Paul did to know Christ. In the widest sense, the effectiveness of the whole Church is affected by whether Christians act like Christians.

The purpose of power is witness, but the purpose of holiness is holiness. The purpose of spirituality is personal—to be like God and so fulfill the ultimate purpose of God, His supreme and original reason for making man, as stated right from the beginning: "Let us make man in our image" (Gen. 1:26). God has business with each of us personally, not merely as His servants or instruments. He loves us, but not because we are useful to Him. You and I don't have relationships with our hammers and chisels. Neither does God have a relationship with us as His tools. Being used by God is simply one of the benefits, a privilege of knowing Christ.

The failure of believers under the attacks of Satan is common. Some people sin openly and conceal their goodness. Others sin secretly while maintaining an appearing of goodness. Paul wrote, "Judge nothing before the appointed time" (1 Cor. 4:5). We are not qualified to preempt the judgment of the all-wise, all-knowing God. Some sins are the wounds of awful battles in which victories were won. Some men fight more temptation in a day than others do in a month. And big men can sin in a big way, a small fault becoming magnified through the lens of fame.

Living with True Confidence

Let us consider the example of the apostle Peter. He was a man of action, but this virtue was also his failing—his impulse to act was too often unrestrained. He spoke when he shouldn't have. He was full of enthusiasm and confidence. When he heard Jesus talk about being taken by His enemies, Peter played the big man, the hero, the protector of his Master (see Matt. 16:21,22). Taking Jesus under your wing is quite an undertaking! Asking Jesus to put His trust in you, imagine that! That is braggadocio, cockiness—self-confidence, if you like. That was Peter—then.

The true beginning of self-confidence is placing your confidence fully in Jesus. Lose confidence in Him and sooner or later your own boastings will burst and look as sorry as pricked balloons. When Jesus was arrested and tried, Peter was amazed to find himself shrinking. He became the shrinking man, so small that the words of a servant girl frightened him. So he put on an act, pretending to be like every other man around. He warmed himself at a fire with other godless characters and became one of them, cursing and swearing, denying that he had anything to do with Jesus of Nazareth (see Matt. 26:74; Mark 14:54). Now, for a failure of that magnitude many a ministerial conference would have defrocked Peter and withdrawn his credentials as an apostle.

When Jesus first called Peter, He said, "Follow me" and gave him a marvelous catch of fish (see Matt. 4:19). Then came three wonderful years with Christ, until the Cross ended them. That brought Peter crashing down, a fall from great heights. Those marvelous days with Jesus seemed to vanish like a mirage. Peter just shrugged his shoulders and went back to square one, back to what he knew: fishing. That, however, was where Jesus had first stepped into his life and called him. And that was where Jesus stepped in *again*. Jesus met Peter fishing again—the same Jesus as yesterday, today and forever. He worked the same miracle, a great catch of fish. And then Jesus again said the words He had said three years before: "Follow me!" (John 21:19). *"For the gifts and calling of God are irrevocable"* (Rom. 11:29, *NKJV*, emphasis mine).

Ephesians tells us that God gave some to be evangelists (see Eph. 4:11). We may talk about the evangelism department of a church or Christian organization, but God does not recognize departments. He only recognizes the Church. *The Church is the evangelism department—all of it.* But evangelism requires more than evangelists; the job needs apostles, teachers, prophets and pastors—*all* of them. What for? To nurture converts. There's nothing wrong with evangelistic crusades, but there could be something seriously wrong afterwards. Jesus said to the disciples from the beach, "Bring some of the fish you have just caught" (John 21:10). Not only evangelists were included in that command.

The thing that strikes us as curious in this scene of Peter's restoration is this: Jesus did not repeat what He had said before about giving Peter the Holy Spirit or the keys of the Kingdom.

He said, "Feed my sheep" (John 21:16,17). Nothing to do with fishing now, but sheep. We eat fish, but sheep must be fed.

Church critics have a saying: "Evangelists make decisions, but Jesus said, 'Make disciples.'" But evangelists *don't* make decisions. It is the converts who make them. Evangelists make nothing. They simply call attention to Christ and work for a response. An evangelist gets responses, but pastors are needed to make disciples. The evangelist brings in the raw material and the pastor has to work with it. However thorough the evangelist is in his ministry, making disciples takes time and cannot be done in a six-day crusade. Some pastors don't manage it in *years*. Jesus spent three years with the Twelve and they were not all that marvelous even then. No evangelist could ever feed new people into the Church, all born again and trained in the principles of discipleship. If he could, pastors and teachers would not be needed.

Incidentally, the Church does not choose and appoint apostles, pastors, teachers and evangelists. The Lord does that. We may appoint others and miss the Lord's appointees. The Catholic Church rejected Martin Luther. The Anglican Church rejected John Wesley. The Methodists rejected William Booth. The Baptists rejected William Carey. The Holiness people rejected William Seymour. But God did not reject any of them.

God has put pastors in every church of any size. They are all part of the leadership, as we call it, helping "those able to help others" (1 Cor. 12:28). They have a heart for people, to care, to visit, to pray. They are God's backroom team of nurses and doctors. The Bible talks about people being "joined together" (Eph. 2:21), the original Greek referring to the setting of a dislocated or broken bone. God has chose these leaders and given them wisdom to counsel.

The pastors *we* choose may have none of these characteristics. We tend to be drawn to businessmen, popular figures, organizers, managers, perhaps generals or even sergeant majors. The true work rests upon those with a gentle and compassionate heart, those ready to put themselves out at any time, largely unknown, young or old, men or women. Their gift is an instinct to recognize troubled faces. They may have a word of knowledge to share with those in need. Or maybe they have a word of knowledge and say nothing to anybody but go and pray.

I don't see how any evangelist can create a church in just a few days, supplying a whole body of people converted out of the streets and fully qualified as disciples. Evangelism is only the first step, not the complete process. To be the kind of man who could do it all in a six-day crusade, he would have to be a kind of guru. An evangelist should not take on the role of a guru with a following. Some pastors are fearful of an evangelist creating that kind of situation in his church, a fear that sadly has not always been unfounded.

Faith Works by Love

Make every effort to add to your faith goodness; and to goodness, knowledge; and to knowledge, self-control; and to self-control, perseverance; and to perseverance, godliness; and to godliness, brotherly kindness; and to brotherly kindness, love. . . . Possess these qualities in increasing measure (2 Pet. 1:5-8).

As I have said, faith is the key, but spirituality must be developed. Spirituality is the quality which will be recognized in heaven and give us our reward or status. It is composed of a lifetime's living, overcoming, putting spiritual things before the carnal.

In the above passage, Peter is not saying that one virtue is derived from another—e.g., self-control from knowledge or perseverance from self-control. We don't progress from one quality to another but should have them all in "increasing measure." Faith does not ultimately lead to love, but rather faith and love are in harness: Faith works by love.

When Jesus restored Peter He did not say, "OK, you are forgiven. Forget the past. Just get on with your work." He said, "Peter, do you love me?" (see John 21:15,17). Peter's love for Christ was the first and the last question. Really it is the *only* question. He won't ask us how many souls we have won. He will only measure us by our love. His words are still "Do you love me?" Well, do we?

PREACHING JUDGMENT TO A POLITICALLY CORRECT WORLD

He sent for Paul and listened to him as he spoke about faith in Christ Jesus. As Paul discoursed on righteousness, self-control and the judgment to come, Felix was afraid (Acts 24:24,25).

Paul was the first missionary to Europe. Wherever he went there he met people whose ideas ran counter to the gospel; their minds had been conformed to a different pattern. All indications were that Europe represented hard, infertile soil, impossible for planting the seeds of the gospel. Paul's encounter with Felix was typical. Christianity was met with fear and suspicion because it represented a new way of looking at everything.

What was so new about Christianity? For one thing, it wasn't just "religion" as usual. The Greeks and Romans served many gods, but those gods did not have the power to change one's entire life. One could practice the rites, make the requisite sacrifices, but Christianity was a new way of thinking—a new way of life. In fact, Felix knew it as The Way. Paul was introducing a revolutionary way of knowing God that changed attitudes and everything about how people lived day to day.

Even though he was raised strictly Jewish, Paul was called by Jesus Himself to preach the gospel to the ethnically and religiously diverse Gentiles, the non-Jewish people of the Greco-Roman world (see Acts 22:21). The Gentiles of Paul's day were devoted to many different philosophies and belief systems. The book of Acts specifically mentions practitioners of magic arts (see 8:9; 19:19), belief in the classical gods (see 14:11), fortune-telling and divination (see 16:16), idol worship (see 17:16), Stoic and Epicurean philosophy (see 17:18) and goddess worship (see 19:27). Also widely and actively practiced were Emperor worship, the occult Orphic mystery religion, the fertility rites of the Eleusinian cults, the Oracles at Dephi and others. Even the Jewish community was divided religiously. The party of the Sadduccees denied important aspects of the supernatural, while the Pharisees affirmed them (see Acts 23:7,8). The Essenes, in an attempt to escape the evil world system, carved out ascetic communities in the wilderness. Other Jews became influenced by Greek thought and culture.

Today this is what we call a pluralistic society. Paul was taking the gospel to people whose entire upbringing and outlook was alien to and even opposed the basic principles upon which the gospel was founded.

Every religion offers a superficial lifestyle, but true Christianity offers much more. For example, Muslim clerics and religious police regulate the way their followers eat, wash, dress, conduct relationships and pray, going to great lengths to enforce their rules. The Bible properly understood does nothing of the sort. True Christianity simply changes the principles of life. Everything becomes motivated by our love for Christ. A born-again person looks at the world through different eyes from the moment he or she opens them (see 2 Cor. 5:14-17).

In many countries, Christians find their way of life clashes with the religions and cultures around them, often resulting in the cruel persecution of believers. Some other religions are specifically opposed to American and European culture; Muslim extremists call America the "Big Satan." Today, the problem of communicating the gospel to groups from different religious backgrounds faces just about any who witness for Christ at home or abroad. In my case, it is a daily issue as I preach to mixed multitudes. We have produced 100 million books and booklets in a hundred different languages in an attempt to build bridges to non-Christians. Often the problem we face is that in many cultures an individual is closely identified with his country or community by his religion. To convert is almost like an act of betrayal. This is especially true in Islamic nations where conversion to Christianity carries an actual death penalty!

However, pluralism is not just a missionary problem anymore. Since World War II, a new demographic has arisen in America and in Europe. The Germans, French, British, Americans and others have undergone significant population changes as immigrants from Asia and the Middle East have flooded in. The West has had to adjust as the new cultures are not integrating with our native and Christian traditions. Pluralism creates friction and in America, amid the rise of tolerance and political correctness, legislation has been adopted to ease the tension.

What We Are Up Against

Acts 24:4,5 illustrates Paul's approach to presenting the gospel to those from different national backgrounds. Felix was a procurator of Judea, but had possibly once been a slave. By breeding he was Roman, but his wife Drusilla was a Jewess. He did have some knowledge of Christianity, possibly through his wife. How the apostle presented the gospel to this pagan ruler is interesting and instructive.

He talked to Felix about four things: (1) faith in Christ, (2) righteousness, (3) self-control and (4) the judgment to come. In this book, I have said much about three of these subjects, and now we come to the fourth. How should we as Christians approach the topic of judgment in a pluralistic, politically correct society?

Today evangelism, or missions, is a net cast across many nations, languages, religions and ways of thinking. When the first modern missionaries worked in India and Africa, they tried to impose Western ways upon converts, as if the Western way of life were the Christian way of life. The first modern missionaries were mainly British—John Wesley was originally a missionary to American Indians. They built British churches, taught British forms of worship and British hymns and provided native cultures with British clothes.

Early missionaries created enormous problems for themselves by trying to westernize their converts. In these faraway lands, Christianity came to be identified with the West, a foreign religion. It is still thought in some areas to be a foreign import. On the other hand, Hudson Taylor believed that faith in Christ could express itself in any cultural form—Christ belongs to all nations. In China, faith in Christ was being presented in a British form, but Hudson Taylor believed that was a mistake. So, he adopted Chinese fashions in order to reach the Chinese. It was a start.

Gospel converts need not change their national cultures, except where they are demonic cultures based on spirit worship. A Chinese Christian culture or Indian Christian culture is just as legitimate as a Western culture. In any case, it is a mistake to think of Western culture as completely Christian. For example, the earliest practice of democracy is pre-Christian, originating in ancient Greece, not in the Bible. And our vast credit economy in the West is not specifically Christian, but we live and serve God within it.

Today the problem of spirituality is being tackled in various ways by people of different beliefs and backgrounds. For example, some try to reconcile themselves and their beliefs to the gospel by claiming that Christianity is not unique, but in essence is the same as all religions; that it is just a matter of common experience. They are trying to settle on what that common experience really is, the "inner light" we all share. After all, it is not politically correct to claim Christianity is unique.

Another pluralistic method is to find the best bits from all religions and put them together—an approach we call syncretism. Others look to the Eastern mystics to develop their religious consciousness, tuning into outside influences. No creeds, no doctrines, not even worship—just feelings of elevation.

In America, religion often means no more than the experience that comes from sitting in a church—the sensation of the place itself, with its quietness, peace and mystery. The liturgy aims to enhance the same psychological effect and often the sermon is an interlude of easy platitudes.

There is a movement afoot in the Church to have "dialogue" with foreign religions. It is said there is light in them all. This worries me. I don't mind dialogue if it means I can tell somebody about Jesus, and I will listen to another's religious beliefs. But often the idea is to interact and integrate. How can we adapt Christianity and its practices to fit in with Buddhism, Islam or Hinduism? This is compromise, which is not only unacceptable but impractical. You can't put all religions into a melting pot and create a stronger alloy; it never works. You only end up with a ragbag stuffed with nonsensical religious odds and ends.

Christianity, however, is a dogmatic religion. The gospel makes hard statements that must be accepted. Christianity is historic; it is fact. The gospel evokes feelings, but it can't be reduced to feelings. It is the truth, whatever people may feel. People have died at the stake not for feelings, but for truth. We must boldly declare the truth and never compromise or dilute it to spare anybody's feelings.

I know we can find grains of gold in the sand. There may be found elements of good even in false faiths. But not all that is good saves, and not all truth is *saving* truth. Good advice and wise maxims won't bring forgiveness. Jesus didn't come to give us advice, dispense knowledge or teach us to find our inner light. He came so that we might have LIFE and more abundantly.

If all religions are the same, we may as well stay home. Let Muslims be Muslims then. Hindus, Brahmins, Buddhists, animists, spiritists, witches—let them stay that way. *But all religions are not the same!* Millions are slighted, not blessed, by their religions. Often their sacred practices produce evils and backward conditions—the oppression of women, intolerance, revenge, fanaticism and enslavement of lower classes, among others. The gospel, on the other hand, is a liberating and uplifting power! Wherever it is accepted, it brings about social improvement of every kind and respect toward the lowest and the least. Remember the words of Isaac Watts's great hymn "Jesus Shall Reign":

Blessings abound wherever He reigns,
The prisoner leaps to lose his chains,
The weary find eternal rest,
And all the sons of want are blessed.

There are millions waiting and hoping for something more, something better than nice feelings. After 30 years among non-Christian peoples, I know that earthbound souls long for something that is found only in Jesus Christ. They want a higher reality, something substantial—more than pomp, ceremonies, observances, prayers and symbols. They want a faith that will be a rock in the storm.

People want to know there is justice in the world; I preach Christ, the Judge of all. They want a power to overcome evil in their own hearts; I preach that Jesus saves. They want forgiveness of sins; I preach that through this man, Christ Jesus, "is preached unto you the forgiveness of sins" (Acts 13:38, KJV). They want to experience God; I preach the baptism of the Holy Spirit filling them mind, body and spirit. They want help in their daily struggles, not a religion that imposes more duties; I preach a Jesus to whom they can hand over their lives, who will take over responsibility for their past, present and future. Who else can do all that? Jesus is truly the only Savior. He has no rival, living or dead.

Christ doesn't set down rules for eating and washing and praying. He changes our basest instincts. His wisdom is planted in us as a law of nature—our new nature in Christ. We are born again; we have divine genes. Our DNA, the double-helix spiral encoded in our genes, guides the growth and characteristics of our physical bodies. DNA is like a tape recording automatically instructing each living cell what it should do. The Spirit of God acts as our spiritual DNA, developing and guiding our growth in Christ.

Preaching the Gospel in a Pluralistic World

The apostles preached judgment. True, this was not a subject the pagans thought about very much. Nevertheless, it was truth and the apostles were sent to preach the truth. This year I have preached to hundreds of thousands of Muslims and Hindus. I make no bones about preaching the whole gospel. I gladly preach Jesus, righteousness, temperance and the coming judgment.

This gospel flames into people's hearts like a sudden dawn after a dark, gloomy night. Jesus is a rock of assurance for a world adrift in a sea of uncertainty. God has not left us trying to cling to cloudy sentiments, grasping at passing wisps of hope. Our Christian message to a confused world is positive, solid and rational.

I don't criticize other beliefs. I don't intentionally offend followers of other religions. I don't argue about religion or dispute as to which belief system is right. I simply present this glorious gospel of Christ positively. If my listeners think their Hindu gods or Allah or Buddha can offer them forgiveness, give them power over sin, clothe them in righteousness and give them hope when it comes to judgment, then fine. Let them go on as they have been. But I know and they know there is nothing like that in their creeds and customs. Only Jesus saves! Nobody else is in the market.

If it is ethics people want, the Word of God is complete. Our Christian ethics come from the Bible. We have no need to go to the Koran or the Hindu myths for guidance. "His divine power has given us everything we need for life and godliness through our knowledge of [Jesus Christ]" (2 Pet. 1:3).

All religions have some theory about how ultimate justice will be accomplished. It is a basic tenet. That is why Jesus said so much about it. He said, "The Father judges no one, but has entrusted all judgment to the Son" (John 5:22). Judgment is in the hands of Jesus, and what hands they are—scarred by piercing iron, they are hands of mercy. He is the Judge, the One who loves us. The name of Jesus brings relief to hearts the world over.

Notice that the apostles did not *threaten* with judgment; it was part of the good news. They did not set out to arouse fears. The apostles had no need to warn people that without Christ they would perish. The people knew very well already that they were perishing. They were already full of fear about what would happen to them, especially at death. Many believed that when they died they would sink into a dark, dreaded underworld guarded by a terrible three-headed dog called Cerberus. The apostles found that at the mention of death and judgment, the heathen world bowed down, fearful. But these men of God came bearing the message of the Cross and Resurrection, of justice and mercy at the throne of divine grace. *There's nothing wrong with that glorious message!* It is the word for all people, of all faiths, of all cultures, of all times, of all races. We need not compromise such wonderful tidings. We declare the truth, the facts. And facts are stubborn things that everybody in our pluralistic society must face.

By the way, the apostles preached judgment, not hellfire. Their epistles and the sermons in Acts are largely silent on that subject, but are strong on the concept of judgment. The word "hell" is mentioned only a couple of times in the New Testament outside of the Gospels and the book of Revelation. Threatening people with hell has no effect. People today laugh at the idea, as the place has been caricatured so much with flames, sulfur, caves, and devils with forked tails.

In the past, preachers have described agonies in a hell God never devised, even for the worst of His creations. The picture has been overdrawn. The medieval Church dwelled on hell to the point of paranoia. One medieval writer said that unbaptized children would suffer in fires that would become worse and worse every century. Who would listen to such talk these days?

To preach hell (or anything else) two things are needed. First, we must give a proper explanation of what the Bible says and, second, we must preach it like Jesus did—if we can. His voice, like everything He did, was an expression of profound anxiety and infinite love for all His creations. He took no pleasure in warning people of Gehenna. He came to do all He could to prevent people from going there, and it gave Him no pleasure to see people consigned to that place. He pronounced woes with tears in His voice.

THE GOSPEL IS A SURGEON'S KNIFE CUTTING OUT THE CANCER OF SIN. PREACHING MUST HAVE THAT EDGE TO IT.

If we are to see apostolic results, we must have apostolic preaching. In the dark regions where I so often preach, any other kind of preaching would be a scandalous betrayal of what the gospel is and a betrayal of those who listen to me. My gospel is the gospel of Jesus, Paul, Peter and company. No matter what beliefs your listeners have been brainwashed with, the gospel is applicable. The gospel deals with the fundamental issues in everyone's life. The gospel is the surgeon's knife cutting out the cancer of sin. Preaching must have that edge to it—"sharper than any double-edged sword" (Heb. 4:12)—and deal honestly and positively with sin, judgment, righteousness, the salvation of the

Cross and the power of God. It is not open for debate. It is for proclamation.

How Jesus Linked His Message with the Last Things

Judgment was a weighty part of Christ's teaching; it solemnized all He had to say. Sometimes He spoke of it explicitly, but it was there all the time implicitly. Eternity is always in view in His teaching. The last things *should* be part of the gospel package. They were when Christ preached it, and it is mainly from Him that we receive our direct knowledge of the final days.

It is startling to see how judgment permeated everything Jesus talked about. He did not come here so that everybody would have a good time partying with the Messiah. He spoke directly about reward and punishment. I think the Church generally soft-peddles judgment today. But it is an essential part of Christ's teachings. He had great compassion, but He never disguised the truth. Out of pity He showed us clearly that judgment is coming.

The necessary fact of judgment brought Him to this planet and took Him to the Cross. Of all human knowledge, that is the supreme fact. He felt such compassion for the multitudes that He fed 5,000 of them and then told them what their fate would be unless they believed on Him. We must give our thoughts to something more than bread, and we must trust Him to save us. Nobody else will.

Jesus on Judgment

From that time on Jesus began to preach, "Repent, for the kingdom of heaven is near" (Matt. 4:17).

This is the first we hear of the Lord's ministry. But John the Baptist preached the same message before Jesus (see Matt. 3:2). It has even been suggested that Jesus began as a·disciple of the Baptist, but I see no evidence of that in Scripture.

However, the message of John was full of judgment, as was that of Jesus. John used expressions like "flee from the coming wrath" (Matt. 3:7) and "every tree that does not produce good fruit will be cut down and thrown into the fire" (v. 10) and "His winnowing fork is in his hand, and he will clear his threshing floor, gathering his wheat into the barn and burning up the chaff with unquenchable fire" (v. 12).

Jesus took up that kind of warning throughout His ministry and used similar figures of speech. But Jesus never threatened; He simply described what is bound to happen, the inevitable. There is no escape—except in Christ. To reject Christ and work wickedness immediately places a person under the wrath of God. Judgment is a matter of cause and effect. One day our life's work will be judged. Our deeds will either stand or collapse; either be swept away in a final flood or remain to our credit forever. The Bible looks beyond the daily concerns and stresses of this world to show us a higher reality—it is eternity that matters.

When Christ was born, eternity broke into the confines of time and space. Heaven has dealings with earth and the judgments of God have already begun to work. Scripture reveals the nature of the forces that shape human destiny. Our temporal world must take account of the eternal. The Sermon on the Mount is an exhortation to live every day in the light of things to come.

That truth should make this world a better place. Awareness of future judgment will bring justice now by making people anxious to do what they know would please the Lord. When preached, the future judgment of God has tangible effects in the present.

Evangelist D. L. Moody once preached to some workmen on strike. He was criticized for this. There were those who claimed that Moody had taken the side of the bosses, that he was encouraging the workers to accept poor wages because their real wages would be given them later in heaven. Moody's critics distorted the gospel message. If we live in the light of the fact that we shall face the righteous Judge, we will fight for what is right and not encourage people to sit silent under injustice. The gospel lifts the lower classes and gives them dignity. It changes nations—always for the better. The gospel is the greatest elevating force ever known!

Jesus on Salvation

Jesus talked of salvation but made it clear what God saves us *from*. It is futile to preach that Jesus saves if people are not in danger—or if they don't *know* they are in danger. The fact that they *do* stand in danger is a truth which must be part of our gospel preaching. Faith in Christ will rescue us from sin, judgment and eternal loss. When sharing the gospel, we are talking about nothing less than a question of human destiny.

The Gospel of John records two elements of Christ's teaching: promise and warning. In these passages, Jesus expounds on His power to save and what will happen if we go unsaved:

Whoever believes in the Son has eternal life, but whoever rejects the Son will not see life, for God's wrath remains on him (John 3:36).

A time is coming when all who are in their graves will hear his voice and come out—those who have done good will rise to live, and those who have done evil will rise to be condemned (John 5:28,29).

Judgment was never far from Christ's mind. In the second of these two passages, Jesus had just healed a man who had been an invalid for 38 years. Miraculously, this man could walk for the first time in four decades, and yet this led to Jesus speaking of people rising from death to face condemnation! Such talk almost seems out of place, but so much He taught related to the judgment to come.

For example, when He heard that a wall had fallen and killed 18 people and that Pilate's soldiers had killed a number of Galileans, Jesus expressed little in the way of sympathy. Instead He remarked, "Unless you repent, you too will all perish" (Luke 13:3,5). Our reaction might be to say how sad it was and promise to say a prayer for the bereaved. But to Christ, the real tragedy was sin and impenitence. A far worse fate loomed for the unrepentant. Jesus took the opportunity while people were still shocked to speak of the greatest tragedy of all: people dying in their sins.

Judgment in Apostolic Evangelism

We will all stand before God's judgment seat (Rom. 14:10).

There are many powerful expressions of judgment throughout the New Testament. Revelation 20:11 speaks of the great white throne of judgment. Hebrews 9:27 says, "Man is destined to die once, and after that to face judgment." When Paul spoke to Felix and Drusilla, he discoursed on "righteousness, self-control and the judgment to come" (Acts 24:25). Pretty bold and straightforward preaching with only two people in the congregation! There could be no doubt to whom Paul was referring.

All the New Testament writers declared that sin brings bitter wages. Some wicked people may seem to have a good time, but nobody gets away with it in the end. We will die in our sins unless we repent and cast ourselves upon the mercy of Christ. Sin *must* be paid for. Sin leads to judgment; they cannot be separated. That is where Christ steps in and pays our debt, suffering the consequences on our behalf.

The Scriptures usually don't declare directly that the wicked are destined to perish. More often we find positive statements that those who trust Christ will *not* perish. In these cases it is only implied that people who don't trust in Christ will perish. There are passages, of course, which say clearly that the unrighteous and unbelievers are under condemnation, but we often can only draw the inference. Why is that?

The reason is that Jesus Christ came to save us from destruction. If we refuse Christ, we have refused the remedy, our way of escape. Christ came to help us, and if we turn Him down, we shall simply get what was coming to us.

People have always known they are to perish. Jesus and the apostles had no need to tell them, nor do we. But the gospel offers hope; it is the answer to the universal dread of death and hopelessness.

Throughout the Roman world at the time of Christ, death was known as the king of terrors. Generally, death was thought to mean a subexistence among the shadows of the underworld. Personality perished and even strong men and warriors existed as mere specters—weak, bloodless, gibbering and squeaking. This is a fate Jesus said would never overtake those who trusted in Him. Instead His own would have eternal life—everlasting robust reality.

By the time of Christ, most of Israel did believe in life after death. They talked of Abraham's Bosom as the place of the dead. "Hades" referred to the state of the dead—they existed. Israel's teachers, the scribes and rabbis, said that unless people knew the law they were cursed (see John 7:49).

Outside Israel, the accepted idea was "Eat, drink and be merry for tomorrow you die."[1] Many didn't even believe they had a soul. On the other hand, the Egyptians had a morbid obsession with death and spent vast fortunes trying to ensure that in some way or other they would prosper in the great beyond.

We are told in the Bible that the apostle Paul disputed with the Stoics, to whom death meant virtual annihilation (see Acts 17:18). Stoic belief was that at death, the spirit of man went back to the great ocean of spirit, like a raindrop into the ocean. They regarded talk of resurrection as "babbling."

Buddhists today have similar expectations. Others believe in reincarnation: the soul returning, perhaps thousands of times, until again the soul finally sinks into the ocean of nothingness. It is released from the burden of existence by ceasing to exist.

In the *Paedo* of Plato, Socrates spends his last hours trying to reason what will happen to him when death comes. He says, "Nothing can harm a good man, either in life or death." But his last words show a pathetic attachment to the superstitions of his day. His dying words: "Crito, we ought to offer a cock to Asclepius. See to it, and don't forget it."[2]

Christians think of the soul as themselves in the fullest sense of personality. The ancient Greeks had no idea of such a soul—the essence of their personality—living on after their death. To them the soul was only a ghostly remnant. To die was to become a thing, not a person.

The promise of Christ is that we will never perish. Salvation is the certainty of life with Christ after death, and of resurrection—an entirely new view of life and death to the ancient world. The saved are kept in the hands of a mighty Savior who had overcome death. It means there is Somebody at the door of death who is able to take care of us. What a mighty salvation! What a mighty Savior—a light in the darkness and a sheltering rock amid the uncertainty of life!

In the West, the gloom of uncertainty overshadows millions, including the rich, the prominent and the powerful. They admit to being troubled and fearful in the face of the future. As the Baby Boomers in America grow older, they become aware they are perishing, "like water spilled on the ground which cannot be gathered up again" (2 Sam. 14:14, NKJV). As they experience the onset of illness and feebleness, they feel themselves fading away, like a candle flame guttering into oblivion. If the gospel means anything at all, it means a cure for this morbid outlook.

> Our Savior, Christ Jesus . . . has destroyed death and has brought life and immortality to light through the gospel (2 Tim. 1:10).

The gospel is salvation and hope. I do not know any religion or any philosophy in the world that offers such hope, and yet it rings true with the human soul.

Christ transformed death. To those who believe, death is no longer a punishment. On the contrary, "Blessed are the dead who die in the Lord" (Rev. 14:13). "Precious in the sight of the LORD is the death of His saints" (Ps. 116:15). Death is no longer left to speculation. We will not perish like a tree rotting in the soil, blasted by storm and lightning. We are saved. We live in Him! Hallelujah!

As we move into the third millennium, human knowledge has advanced far beyond anything we could have predicted just 200 years ago. Technology makes the "impossible" happen every hour in every home. But the same old problems remain with us: wickedness, fear, judgment, sickness.

In the past two centuries, thousands of new religions, small and large, have been founded; but not one of them has an answer to the problem of sin and fear and no clue about the righteous judgment of a holy God. Ten thousand new ideas have been presented to explain the universe, but they all fail to solve the plight of mankind, to save us from ourselves.

The gospel does not fail. It is the revelation of God in His Son, Jesus Christ. When we look to Him, we are never disappointed. He strides across the centuries as the one and only Savior and His feet are firmly planted in the new millennium.

Paul wanted to preach in Rome. He said he would not be ashamed of the gospel, even in the hub of the pagan empire. I want to preach in the new millennium—anywhere—and I will not be ashamed of the gospel, for it is still the power of God unto salvation to everyone who believes.

A Final Word

One day the last hymn will be sung, the final message preached and the closing prayer offered. Judgment *will* come. The saints of God, lost sheep who were found by the Savior and Lord Jesus Christ and who followed Him home, will go to their heavenly reward. What a day that will be!

It will be an unparalleled opportunity to meet the Master face-to-face, to appreciate the beauties of heaven, to rejoice in fellowship with God's family and learn more about our eternal destiny. It will all seem so right, so timely, the hope of the ages fulfilled. But then it will be too late to evangelize; there will be no spiritually lost sheep in heaven.

"Now is the day of salvation" (2 Cor. 6:2).

Notes

1. The Romans held beliefs similar to those of the Greeks. A person once dead was thought to cross the River Styx into a vast, confused space, never to return. During the festival of Dionysius, the spirits of the dead were allowed to return and walk in the streets. People smeared their doorways with pitch to keep them out and when the day ended, they were all sent back to Hades as everybody shouted, "Get out, hobgoblins! The Athnesteria is over." Source: Louise B. Zaidman, Pauline Schmitt Pantel and Paul Carledge, *Religion in the Ancient Greek City* (Cambridge, Mass.: Cambridge University Press, 1993), p. 77.

2. Asclepius was the mythical god of medicine. The cock was considered sacred in his temples.

Other Books
by Reinhard Bonnke

Over 105,000,000 books and booklets by Reinhard Bonnke in over 123 languages have been printed in over 45 countries of the world. Powerful evangelistic messages and solid teaching characterize his writing and have inspired and changed the lives of many.

- *Evangelism by Fire*
- *Mighty Manifestations*
- *Faith, The Link with God's Power*
- *How to Have Assurance of Salvation*
- *The Secret of the Power of the Blood of Jesus*
- *The Holy Spirit Baptism*
- *How to Receive a Miracle from God*
- *The Lord Your Healer*
- *First of all ... Intercession*
- *Redemption, the Romance of Redeeming Love*
- *Faith for the Night*
- *Four Keys to Victory*
- *Explosion of Life*
- *From Minus to Plus*
- *The Ultimate Plus*

For further information about the ministry of Reinhard Bonnke or Christ for all Nations, please visit our web site on the internet or contact the office nearest to you:

USA: Christ for all Nations
PO Box 590588, Orlando, FL32859-0588
Phone: 1(407) 2517000

Canada: Christ for all Nations
Box 25057, London, Ontario, N6C 6A8
Phone: 1(519) 4325723

Website: http://www.cfan.org

Other Books
by Reinhard Bonnke

Evangelism by Fire
A book to fan the spark of evengelism into a blazing furnace! Here lies the true heartbeat of Reinhard Bonnke. It is impossible to read this Holy Spirit inspired book without being gripped by God's urgency to reach the lost of this generation.

- Ideal for pastors, leaders, students
- Over 800,000 in print
- 266 pages
- 16 page color photo section
- Workbook available

Mighty Manifestations
A book to challenge the believer to step out and use the "power tools of God", the gifts of the Holy Spirit. All the gifts are covered in detail. Reinhard Bonnke shows how we can be effective in using the gifts we have been given.

- Ideal for pastors, leaders, students
- 236 pages
- 16 page color photo section
- Workbook available

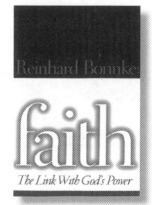

Faith... the Link with God's Power
Reinhard Bonnke draws from his years of personal study and ministry to millions to reveal that Faith is the fertile ground in which God moves and that it is not the size of your faith, but the size of the God you believe in that determines the results. Faith is like a wiring system that carries power into our lives. Faith itself is not the power, but it links us to the power source. There is no link to God's power without faith.

- New!
- 283 pages

Booklets
by Reinhard Bonnke

How to have Assurance of Salvation

This booklet tackles the first and most vital crisis that every new believer faces. Before anything else, we must know we are saved! It is the crucial link between salvation and discipleship. Using graphic illustrations from Scripture, this message forms the basis of the booklet Now that you are Saved, given to new believers in every CfaN campaign.

* For new or uncertain believers
* Approx 26 pages

The Secret of the Power of the Blood of Jesus

The blood type of Jesus is unique. Since it was spiritually created it has spiritual power. As a young evangelist Reinhard Bonnke vowed that wherever he went he would preach on the blood of Jesus. This booklet contains that powerful gospel message in all its life-changing anointing.

* Excellent for open-air evangelism or as a gift for unsaved friends
* Approx 26 pages

The Holy Spirit Baptism

The greatest assurance of all flows from personal experience of the manifestation of God's power. Drawing from Scripture, this carefully explained and simple to understand booklet brings the believer to the place of faith where he or she can receive the Baptism of the Holy Spirit. Common misconceptions are answered and the reader is challenged to ask and receive!

* Approx 28 pages

How to Receive a Miracle from God

Perhaps the greatest single obstacle to accepting the reality of miracles is our inability to understand God's dynamics. The dynamics of the miraculous are the Word of God, Faith and Obedience. When these three are in place, miracles happen. This booklet will unlock the doors of unbelieving hearts to expect a miracle from God.

* Approx 24 pages

Other booklets in this series
* The Lord Your Healer • First of all...Intercession
* Redemption, the Romance of Redeeming Love • Faith for the Night